The Power of Questions

A Guide to Teacher and Student Research

Beverly Falk and
Megan Blumenreich

HEINEMANN
Portsmouth, NH

Heinemann

A division of Reed Elsevier Inc.

361 Hanover Street

Portsmouth, NH 03801–3912

www.heinemann.com

Offices and agents throughout the world

Library of Congress Cataloging-in-Publication Data

Falk, Beverly.
    The power of questions : a guide to teacher and student research / Beverly Falk and Megan Blumenreich.
        p. cm.
    Includes bibliographical references and index.
    ISBN 0-325-00698-9 (alk. paper)
    1. Research—Methodology—Study and teaching.   2. Inquiry-based learning.
I. Blumenreich, Megan.   II. Title.
    LB1047.3.F35 2005
    371.39—dc22   2004024036

Editor: Lois Bridges
Production service: Denise Botelho
Production coordinator: Sonja Chapman
Cover design: Night & Day Design
Typesetter: Gina Poirier, Gina Poirier Design
Manufacturing: Steve Bernier

Printed in the United States of America on acid-free paper
09   08   RRD   4   5

This book is dedicated to our parents,
Mollie and Phil Falk
and
Peggy and Gene Blumenreich,
who nurtured and answered our very first questions

● ● ●

Contents

o o o

$\mathcal{A}$cknowledgments

○ ○ ○

*I have learned many things from teachers; I have learned many things
from my friends; and I have learned even more from my students.*

—The Talmud

Our students, both adults and children, have taught us the value of questions. We would like especially to thank our teacher education students at The City College of New York, whose research projects have demonstrated the power of questions to improve learning in urban classrooms. (Please see the list at the end of this section of those whose work is referenced in this book.) Our experience with these prospective and practicing teachers, many of whom grew up in the neighborhoods where they now teach, has deepened our understandings of the importance of research conducted by those who truly understand the contexts they study.

We also want to thank our teacher colleagues—Mark Bushwinka, Susan Gordon, Betty Kouassi, Susan MacMurdy, Linda Margolin, Mercedes Orozco, and Sasha Wilson—whose work is featured in this book. By sharing their thoughts and what they do, they make it possible for others to see images of the learning that can happen when children's questions are honored in the classroom.

We are grateful as well to our own teachers, who have mentored us either directly or through their writings. Among them are Marilyn Cochran–Smith, Linda Darling–Hammond, Eleanor Duckworth, Celia Genishi, Jerome Harste, Elisabeth Hirsch, Ruth Shagoury Hubbard, Ann Lieberman, Nancy Lesko, Susan Lytle, Brenda Miller Power, Marjorie Siegel, and the late Lillian Weber. Their insights have informed our thinking about qualitative research, teaching, and learning, and what it means to be a professional and change agent in education. Their influences are apparent throughout this book.

Acknowledgments

Many thanks are in order to Lois Bridges, our editor at Heinemann, for her patience, encouragement, provocative ideas, and, most important, her unfailing support.

And finally, nothing is possible without colleagues, friends, and family. We thank Al Posamentier, Gretchen Johnson, and Jim Neujahr at The School of Education of The City College of New York, who supported our efforts to teach courses that are responsive to our students' experiences. We are grateful to our City College colleagues Sheila Gersh, Doris Grassebaurer, Alexandra Miletta, and others for sharing information and resources that appear in this book. Thanks also to friend and colleague Meg Campbell for her brainstorming help with the title.

Special love and gratitude goes to our families—Alan, Meryl, Waldo, Luba, and Thabiti (who officially became a family member in the midst of our writing); and Jon, Hank, and Maggie (who we welcomed into the world during this time) for not only tolerating our absences but nurturing us during those long, long hours at the computer.

Teacher colleagues and former students at The City College of New York, The City University of New York, whose work is featured in this book:

Ignacia Almonte
Neurys Bonilla
Yolan Bravo
Hilda Brito
Estelle Cadiz
Jumel Carlos
Shenaz Carmichael
Cristina Castellon
Patricia Edwards
Ryan Flessner
Loretta Francis
Michelle Gill
Angela Goan
Anna Hart
Seung Hee
Bridgette Hozumi
Gina Joseph
Emma Markarian

Nkenge Mayfield
Natalie McCabe
Swati Mehta
Tabitha Perez
Kisha Pressley
Teresa Roman
Sheri Rothman
Nereida Saban
Juliana Sage
Allison Schoen
Yolanda Serrano
Matthew Steinberg
Marlene Streisinger
Melissa Sugrim
Jeannette Tavarez
Michael Zimski
Kathryn Zvokel

One

Making the Case for Teacher Research

○ ○ ○

One of the great things about teaching is that it offers the possibility for a life of continual learning. Not the tedious kind of learning many of us have experienced in school, but the kind of authentic learning that happens along the way of living, what Eleanor Duckworth (1987) calls "the having of wonderful ideas." This is the kind of learning that leads to genuine understanding or mastery of a new skill, that excites and energizes, that stays forever in our minds and our hearts, that leads to new questions and investigations, and is generative of other forms of learning.

Young children experience this kind of learning before they ever step foot in school. Not only have they solved the mystery of their language, they have learned countless things about themselves, their families, and the world around them through their continuous questioning, exploring, experimenting, and investigating. But something happens to this investigative nature as we get older and enter school. The wonder of the early years fades. By the time we enter the fourth or fifth grade, our natural inquisitiveness almost seems to disappear. Somewhere along the way we stop asking about the "how," the "what," and the "why"—questions that lead to deeper thinking—and we grow acculturated to the routine questions that currently dominate the work of schools: How do you spell _____? What is the formula for _____? What is the definition of _____? These kinds of questions generally are external to the learner. Usually presented in isolation from learners' experiences or understandings, they focus on facts that easily fade with time. They so govern the way we learn that we have little opportunity or time to pursue more personally important or in-depth questions (Falk & Margolin, 2005).

In real life, however, the pursuit of personally important questions is what leads to new discoveries, creations, or realizations (Arnold, 1995;

Gardner, 1998). Many educators, over the years, have called for schools to offer better preparation for such experiences: John Dewey wrote of the need for education to begin with "learners' passions and questions" (1963, p. 3); Jean Piaget of how education should nurture citizens to be "capable of doing new things, not simply repeating what others have done" (in Greene, 1978, p. 80); Paolo Freire (1970) of how education should be instrumental in widening horizons, opening perspectives, discovering possibilities, and overcoming obstacles.

In the midst of the complexities of our twenty-first century life, now more than ever we need schools to produce thoughtful questioners and life-long learners. We need to reconfigure teaching to help students tap into their own questions, generate new ideas, pursue their answers, and put their knowledge to use. To do this, we must find ways to reawaken and sustain the excitement of learning from our early years. If we as teachers want to be able to help our students rediscover this desire, we ourselves need to relearn how to investigate, inquire, experiment, and explore. Only by experiencing such learning personally can we come to know and appreciate the challenges, fears, risks, and joys that generating and pursuing meaningful questions can bring.

The research/teaching connection

Good teaching is not merely a technical matter of delivering information from a recipe or text. Rather, it is about coming to know students well— their skills, learning styles, interests, strengths, as well as their areas in need of improvement—so that we can help them make connections between new information and what they already know; connections that make sense and that last. To do this we need to know what our students understand and how these understandings have been shaped by prior knowledge, experiences, and cultural perspectives. We can come to know these critical aspects of learners and learning by making research about our students, our classrooms, our schools, and our practice a regular and systematic part of our teaching lives.

The word *systematic* is used deliberately here because we want to distinguish between systematic research and just casually pursuing a question. A planned inquiry, conducted over time, with clear goals, purposes, and well-defined data sources has the potential to yield information that may not appear in more informal or sporadic examinations of a question. Systematic research about our students and teaching— through observation, documentation, and reflection—can help us to make informed decisions that support our students' development. It can help us to look at what we do in a fresh way. A systematic study also provides a process for us to become aware of any assumptions and biases we carry with us that may affect how we view and resolve our questions.

For example, sometimes we develop images of children based only on memories of a few negative experiences. We may characterize Victor as a troublemaker because we have witnessed him fighting with other children. Or may see Cynthia as bossy because we have seen her telling other children what to do. Yet, if we were to study Victor and Cynthia systematically by regularly observing and documenting their behavior, interviewing them and their family members, or taking photos of them at various times during the school day, we might come to see them in a new light. We might come up with understandings about them that reveal important qualities we have missed. We might find that Victor acts out in ways that produce conflict, but he does this only when he has difficulty expressing his feelings and is so frustrated that he lashes out at anyone in his path. With this additional information we would likely treat him quite differently—not as a troublemaker who has to be continually constrained, but as a child who needs our help to verbalize and act appropriately on what he is thinking. As a result, we might be better able to help change his negative behavior.

Cynthia's bossiness we might also come to see differently. Although it may annoy us that she is always telling children what to do, through careful observation we may come to understand that she has a strong interest in helping others and is quick to catch on to things. Because she has little outlet for these strengths, she expresses them as bossiness. This additional information might help us to transform our characterization of her as bossy into someone with a potential for leadership. As a result we might start to provide opportunities for her to be helpful and to assume new responsibilities.

Systematic investigation can also be used to study a teaching problem or issue. Whether it be studying how to help your fourth graders ask more substantive questions during literature circles, figuring out what to do with the sixth graders who continually disrupt your class, or exploring how to engage the parents of your students who just never seem to participate in anything, careful study of a problem can help you find solutions that have the potential to improve your teaching. (See Figure 1–1.) The study of a problem can begin with a question or it may emerge from evidence you have been collecting about a child or your work. As

Figure 1–1. Using Research to Improve Your Teaching

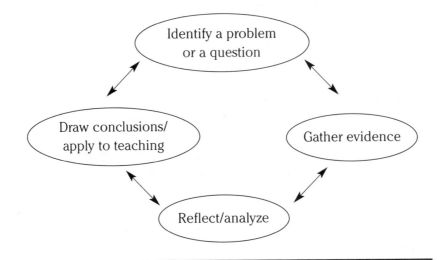

you reflect on what you do and apply new understandings to your teaching, new questions may emerge that require further study. The research process is not linear; it is iterative.

In this book we present a process for how to create a systematic plan of research about your practice. We will take you, reader, through all the steps involved: how to formulate your question, develop a design for your study, investigate what others have learned about the question you want to pursue, use different tools to gather evidence, analyze your findings, write about what you have learned, and share your understandings with others. We call this process *inquiry research* to emphasize its investigative, open-ended nature. Although we present it in a formal way (appropriate for the work of a teacher research course or preparation for a publishable article), you can adapt this process any way that you wish for the investigation you might want to undertake. At each step of the process we offer an analogous model for your work with children so that you can help them, in turn, to become investigators. We also offer related exercises and questions to help you think about your work. And in a accompanying, on-line resource guide for teacher educators, we provide rubrics designed to guide, support, and assess candidates' work. It is our hope that whatever you choose to use will help you to enliven your own teaching life as well as the learning that takes place in your classroom with your students.

Research purposes: Shifts in perspectives

Traditionally, research has been defined as an enterprise outside of the realm of teaching. Conducted by "experts," who historically have been seen as the developers of theories and knowledge, educational research has been used to create policies, curricula, and programs for teachers to pass on to their students. In this conception, teachers (and their students as well) are considered to be passive recipients of other peoples' knowledge, confined to the roles of transmitters, implementers, receivers, or consumers of other peoples' knowledge.

The type of research presented in this book conceptualizes the purpose and participants of research differently—as situated in the lived experience of teaching and learning, as part of the purview of both teachers and students (Chandler–Olcott, 2002; Darling–Hammond, 2001; Feiman–Nemser, 2001; Rock & Levin, 2002). In this conception, teachers and students are considered to be capable of generating their own knowledge by engaging in investigations about issues related to their interests, the curriculum, or their work (Bissex & Bullock, 1987; Cochran–Smith & Lytle, 1990; Erickson, 1986; Florio–Ruane & Walsh, 1980; Lytle & Cochran–Smith, 1989). They are encouraged to be active questioners, doers, and problem solvers who produce knowledge that is both theoretical and practical (Clandinin & Connelly, 1995; Grimmett, 1993). This shift in perspective characterizes research as a process of inquiry that has the potential to yield powerful learning (Wells, 1994; Zeichner, 1994) as well as challenges hierarchical conceptions that have traditionally determined who creates knowledge and what kinds of knowledge are privileged over others (Cochran–Smith & Lytle, 1993; Fine, 1992; McDonald, 1992).

Constructivism: The theory underpinning the process of inquiry

The inquiry process of research is tied to constructivist learning theories that have emerged from advances in cognitive science during the last decades (Windschitl, 2002). Cognitive constructivism, which draws on the theories of Jean Piaget, describes learning as a process in which individuals "construct" new understandings about the world through active engagement with materials, ideas, and relationships. These new understandings are formed when prior knowledge and experience connect with new information (Chandler–Olcott, 2002; Piaget & Inhelder, 1969).

Social constructivism, which draws from the theories of Lev Vygotsky (1978), defines the process of learning construction similarly but focuses especially on how people co-construct knowledge through social interaction. Social constructivism emphasizes the social nature of learning—the facilitative role that others play in the process and the diversity of perspectives on reality that exist.

> In this view, learning cannot be separated from action: perception and action work together in a dialogical manner. And there is no representation of reality that is privileged, or "correct." There are, instead, a variety of interpretations that are used for different purposes in different contexts. (Richardson, 1997, p. 8)

Other understandings about learning that complement and enhance constructivist theories include the notions that people are motivated to learn what is of interest to them (Carini, 1987; Dewey, 1963; Eisner, 1991b; Kilpatrick, 1925), skill and fact learning are best acquired in meaningful contexts (Bruner, 1960), learners have different strengths and "intelligences" that call on teachers to make available different pathways to knowledge (Gardner, 1983), and each individual's potential for growth is limited only by the expectations of her teachers and the opportunities for learning provided to her (Resnick, 1987).

Inquiry as a framework for teaching and learning

These ideas about how people learn have influenced recent conceptions of teaching and learning. Inquiry is becoming valued not as a skill to be learned, but as a framework for education (Short et al., 1996). The teacher's role within this framework is not to transmit knowledge from expert to novice in a uniform way (Burke & Crafton, 1994; Freire, 1970), but rather to help learners actively explore their own questions and cultivate the critical thinking skills on which they will need to draw throughout their lives (Weber, 1991). Teaching within such a framework is more than merely instructing learners how to search for answers to predetermined questions. It is different too from engaging students in interdisciplinary studies predesigned by teachers or curriculum developers (Eisner, 1994; Gardner, 1983; Harste, 1994; Whitin & Whitin, 1996). Rather, a distinguishing and valued feature of teaching within an inquiry framework is to awaken learners' own questions and use these as the driving force for learning (Falk & Margolin, 2005). The goal is to support learners to explore their world through a variety of lenses, adjust or transform their thinking, experiment with tools in their environment, and invent new problems and ideas (Pataray–Ching & Roberson, 2002).

Inquiry as a stance has special significance in the context of the culturally, socioeconomically, and linguistically diverse communities that characterize schools in the world today. These conditions call on teachers to come to the job armed not only with deep knowledge of content, skills, and how children learn, but also to understand how to apply these strategies to the diverse learners and ever-changing situations that are the hallmark of contemporary life. Central to the work of teachers, then, is learning how to put theory into practice and how to problematize and problem solve the complex issues common in schools today.

Teacher inquiry research can help to address these challenges. The process of solving problems with evidence collected through research can help teachers think critically, reflect on their work, connect theory with practice, take charge of their own learning, and take action to make change. Engaging in inquiries can thus help teachers get a feel for what it means to be a questioner, a knower, and a doer. By experiencing themselves as learners in this way, teacher researchers gain an understanding of how to facilitate better their students' learning.

Research for children

Throughout this book, as we discuss how to develop and implement teacher research, we encourage you to reflect on the experience of conducting your own inquiry and consider developing such kinds of projects in your classrooms for your students. We hope that as you experience what it is like to generate your own question, think autonomously about a subject that interests you, construct arguments based on evidence rather than someone else's view of the right answer, and make your own thinking processes explicit, you will be inspired to provide opportunities for your students to do the same.

At this time of high-stakes testing and increased curriculum control at the local, state, and federal levels, developing research projects for children might seem to be moving children away from the "nuts and bolts" of learning at school. However, when one considers the potential for learning that an inquiry project presents, it becomes clear why making the necessary adjustments to fit this type of work into the school day is a worthwhile endeavor. Research projects for children can help them work out ideas, develop theories, solve problems, and articulate their beliefs. Through inquiry they can learn about the importance of using evidence to guide their thinking. As children collect "data" in a variety of ways, they get the opportunity to develop skills in the context of real-life learning experiences. They can develop literacy skills by researching their project in books or on the Internet, by taking "field notes," interviewing, or developing questionnaires. They can use math skills as they find patterns in the data they collect, graph results, or score questionnaires. As they learn to analyze their data, synthesize their findings with the research they have read, and draw conclusions about their projects, they gain first-hand experience with diversity—how there are multiple ways to interpret the world and not always only one right answer. If you want children to become autonomous thinkers who are skilled at both posing and solving problems, building curricula that utilize inquiry research is a useful, appropriate, and rewarding activity.

To help you think about how to incorporate inquiry research into the work of your classroom, here are a few questions on which to reflect:

- How can you orchestrate projects in which your students can explore their own working theories about their lives or the world around them, gather evidence to understand further the issues surrounding these topics, and then reevaluate their initial theories?

- How can you maintain a balance between making sure your students acquire the necessary skills and knowledge to meet district and state standards, and finding time to support your students to follow their own intellectual puzzlements and interests?

- In what ways can you expand on experiences you are currently offering your students to develop their own inquiry work?

Exercise 1: Reflecting on a powerful learning experience

Take a moment to reflect on your life as a learner and try to locate or recollect a powerful learning experience that you have had, one in which you genuinely learned something or had one of those "Aha!" moments that has stayed with you forever. This experience might be recent or may go back to your childhood. It might have taken place either inside or outside of school.

Jot down a few notes about it on a piece of paper. Now try to identify:

- What about this learning experience made it powerful?
- What role did interest play in your learning?
- What kind of support did you have for your learning?
- What are the implications of this experience for teaching children?

Putting Teacher Research
into a Context

○ ○ ◉

Before discussing the details of how to conduct teacher inquiry research, let us put it into a context—explain how it is similar to and different from other kinds of research in its purpose, method, and form.

Experimental versus naturalistic approaches

Most people's notion of research comes from the sciences, where researchers outside the subject of study perform experiments on animals or people to "prove" a hypothesis right or wrong. In this *experimental approach*, researchers isolate the subject of the research in a laboratory or control the conditions of an experiment in a natural setting (this is called quasi-experimental approach) to test the impact of a single variable. Experimental and quasi-experimental research is used to test theories and gather information about trends or the broad impact of issues on large groups to produce understandings that can be generalized (i.e., used by many different people in a variety of contexts). It usually employs *quantitative methods,* meaning it examines issues in ways that are represented by numbers, such as collecting test scores, data sets, or surveys (often on a large scale), and then analyzing them through the use of statistical formulas.

In contrast to this experimental approach, the type of research presented in this book represents a *naturalistic approach.* Instead of taking place in a laboratory, this kind of research is field focused and examines phenomena in their authentic network of relationships within their natural contexts (Eisner, 1991a). Examples of naturalistic research are the work of anthropologist Margaret Mead, who traveled to a small village in distant Samoa to immerse herself in a study of its culture; or the work of naturalist Jane Goodall, who studies primates in their natural habitat in Africa. Studies conducted in the tradition of naturalistic research aim to understand the meaning and nature of the people, places, or situations under investigation; to get to know what the world looks like for those who are being studied—what their lives are like; what kinds of structures, processes, interactions, and relationships shape their existence; what meaning all these things have for them. The goal is not, as in experimental research, to identify and harness variables that will act in predictable ways, to prove a hypothesis right or wrong, or to come up with *yes* or *no* answers that can be generalized to similar situations. Rather, the goal is to shed light on an area that has received little exploration, to gain insights into the particular issue under investigation in its uniqueness as part of a particular context and time, to enhance the reader's understanding of the multiple perspectives and interactions of those who are being studied (Yin, 1984). Meaning is derived in naturalistic research from a sense of how all the parts work together to form a whole (Connelly & Clandinin, 1990).

Naturalistic research tends to examine the objects of study through *qualitative methods* instead of quantitative, meaning it relies primarily for its data not on numbers, but on description and depiction gained from observations, open-ended interviews, photography, videography, and/or document collection. Qualitative methods examine the details of life close-up through a "thick," rich, detailed description that gets beneath the surface of the experience and provides insight into the setting's values, cultural mores, notions, and deep-seated attitudes (Geertz, 1973; Merryfield, 1990; Patton, 1990). Through such an examination of particulars, this kind of research aims to lead the reader to recognize other such particulars in new and foreign contexts, thus leading to a rethinking of the phenomenon being studied, bringing about the discovery of new meaning, and extending the reader's experience and understandings (Merriam, 1988).

Naturalistic research using qualitative methods may investigate the same issue as experimental research using quantitative methods, but it does so in a different form and from a different perspective. Instead of trying to generate proof of a theory through examination of a large sample or group, it seeks only the truth of the particular, looking deeply at a singular phenomenon (Merriam, 1988). Instead of relying on the calculation of numbers to arrive at conclusions, this process is generally interpretive in character, explaining why something is taking place, describing the quality of experience, using expressive language, and often presenting the voices of the various participants in the community under study (Eisner, 1991a). By gaining a deep understanding of the particular

object of study, it provides insights that can inform understandings of
other people, places, or things (see Figure 2–1 for an overview of the
characteristics of these different research approaches).

Different research approaches reflect different paradigms

Research that is descriptive, naturalistic, and interpretive stems from a particular way of looking at the world (often called a *paradigm*). The paradigm from which teacher inquiry research is derived is referred to alter-
nately as either *naturalistic, hermeneutic, constructivist,* or *interpretive.* This
paradigm or frame of reference differs from the paradigm that undergirds
experimental research (often referred to as the *positivist paradigm*) in

Figure 2–1. Qualities of Different Research Approaches

Experimental	**Naturalistic**
Purpose	
Proving a theory	Developing a theory
Determining cause and effect	Probing for understanding/insights
Making generalizations	Seeking the truth of the particular
Verification	Interpretation and analysis
Methods used	
Deductive	Inductive
Quantitative (numbers)	Qualitative (words)
Single method	Multiple methods (triangulated data)
Characteristics	
Focused on variation of isolated variables	Holistic
Context free	Context embedded
Value free	Value laden
Uses particulars to make generalizations	Uses particulars to create flavor, distinctiveness, uniqueness of a situation/person/place
Detached, distant perspective	Insider perspective
Dispassionate voice	Expressive language and presence of voice

regard to how it views the nature of reality (ontology), the nature of knowledge (epistemology), and the methods used to find out what needs to be known (methodology) (Guba & Lincoln, 1989).

The positivist paradigm views reality as singular, independent of any observer or interest, and operating according to immutable laws. In contrast to that way of thinking, the hermeneutic paradigm views reality as a conglomeration of multiple, socially constructed realities. This belief system holds that there is no ultimate, objective truth; that all knowledge is the product of interaction between humans and is therefore problematic, indeterminate, unsettled, and ambiguous. Knowledge is viewed as humankind's best effort to date of making sense out of its situation.

The epistemological question of how we can be sure of what we know also differs according to the different paradigms or belief systems. The positivist paradigm asserts that it is possible for an observer to remain detached and distant from the object being studied, and to leave out any value considerations influencing it. In contrast, the hermeneutic framework asserts that values permeate every paradigm; that every belief is a human construction and is therefore dependent on human values. All aspects of research—the nature of the problem selected for study, the choice of paradigm for carrying out the inquiry, the choice of instrumentation and analysis modes, the choice of interpretations made, and the conclusions drawn—are affected by human values.

> Values must be accorded a central place in human study
> because they come closer to the core of humanness than
> most other characteristics of people. Values provide the
> basis for ascribing meaning and reaching understanding;
> an interpretive, constructivist paradigm cannot do with-
> out them. The safest and most intelligent course is to
> admit that fact and use it to one's advantage. (Guba &
> Lincoln, 1989, p. 102)

Rather than attempting to control one's biases, a researcher who works within a hermeneutic paradigm instead tries to be upfront about his or her biases. Also affected by different belief systems is the method developed to find things out. The positivist paradigm holds that truth can only be seen when the object under study is in isolation, stripped of the contaminating influences of its context. Thus, the experimental approach (as was discussed earlier) is geared toward identifying and harnessing variables that will act on the object of study in predictable ways. The goal is to verify a theory or make generalizations that are time and context free. In contrast, the hermeneutic paradigm asserts that much of knowledge is time and context bound, and can only be looked at in that sense. This approach utilizes a discovery process, often arrived at through the joint construction of meaning made by the many participants in the situation. Its concern is not with verification but with interpretation and analysis.

Validity and reliability

Differing views about these approaches to research generally focus on issues of validity and reliability. *Validity* is a term that refers to whether a study actually describes or measures what it claims to report (internal validity) and whether the findings of the study can be generalized to other situations (external validity). *Reliability* is a term that refers to whether a study will consistently demonstrate the same results. Although the notions of research validity and reliability were originally associated with studies concerned with tests and measurement (Wolcott, 1990), these concepts are also applied to studies that are naturalistic and qualitative. Yet, validity and reliability are issues about which there is great conflict. Although experimental researchers are generally in agreement that validity and reliability are determined on the basis of how significant, replicable, and objective statistical tests of data are, naturalistic, qualitative researchers have many different interpretations of what validity and reliability mean.

To many, the criteria for validity and reliability in naturalistic, qualitative research are the consistency (Merriam, 1988), dependability (Lincoln & Guba, 1985), confirmability, and credibility of the evidence (Yin, 1994). Others would add the coherence, persuasiveness, and cogency of the researcher's argument (Eisner, 1991a). Many qualitative researchers work to achieve these qualities by creating a research design and methods of analysis that are "analytically rigorous and explicitly systematic" (Patton, 1990, p. 462). One way that some qualitative researchers work toward developing rigorous and systematic findings is to *triangulate* the data. At least three (thus the triangle metaphor) different data sources are used to generate the findings of the study. The researcher's analysis searches for trends, patterns, or themes from among the evidence collected (Patton, 1990). Evidence that does not fit leads to alternative views.

Other qualitative or naturalistic researchers aim for validity and reliability by leaving an audit trail—describing in detail how the study was conducted and how the findings were derived from the evidence (Guba & Lincoln, 1981). Still others share their data with readers and reviewers in an attempt to let them draw their own conclusions. Wolcott, for example, writes, "I make a conscious effort to include primary [raw] data in my final accounts, not only to give readers an idea of what my data are like but to give access to the data themselves" (1990, p. 130).

Some qualitative researchers question whether achieving validity in research is even possible. Among those who hold this view, some believe that there is no such thing as objectivity, that researchers' suppositions and interpretations cannot help but influence anything that they study—even when shared as raw data (Cortazzi, 1993). Others question whether there is even such a phenomenon as individual subjectivity. They suggest instead that individuals' points of view are not genuinely their own, but are the products of a complex web of preexisting social influences (Blumenreich, 2001). These different perspectives will be addressed in more practical terms when we discuss how to create a research design in Chapter 5.

How teacher inquiry research fits in

Teacher research is generally situated in the hermaneutic paradigm. It is usually naturalistic and most often relies predominantly on qualitative methods. However, teacher research adds another dimension to the naturalistic approach. Because we teachers have the unique perspective of knowing classrooms and schools intimately, because the questions we investigate are often drawn from the dilemmas of our daily lives, and because in many studies we are "participant observers," meaning that we are both the subject of study as well as the researcher, our investigations offer the potential to contribute useful understandings that outside researchers cannot possibly hope to obtain. In fact, we teachers are often in the best position to study, adapt, and create teaching methods and theories related to the needs of our individual classrooms.

Mixing research paradigms, approaches, and methods

When thinking about the differences between positivist and hermaneutic paradigms, experimental and naturalistic approaches, or quantitative and qualitative methods, it is important to keep in mind that these are on a continuum rather than strict and separate philosophical camps. Researchers frequently lean toward one paradigm and approach but borrow methods from another. For instance, a teacher's examination of her students' experiences with a certain teaching strategy in her classroom, relying predominantly on qualitative data such as in-depth observations, may be at the naturalistic end of the research continuum. The focus of the study might be the children's perspectives of the impact of a particular strategy. However, the strategy's impact on the children's learning might also be examined. For this purpose, quantitative data such as test scores might also be collected and used. Or a study of family involvement that aims to get parents'/caregivers' perspectives on home-school relations by collecting qualitative data from in-depth interviews with a select group of parents/caregivers in one class, could also gather quantitative data from a true/false survey administered to all the parents/caregivers in that class to provide more general understandings about the thinking of the wider group.

Research approaches and methods are sometimes mixed at the other end of the research continuum as well. Quasi-experimental or what is often referred to as "process-product research" is an example of such mixing. This type of research is research *on* teaching, rather than teacher research. Driven by methods derived from the field of psychology rather than the field of anthropology (the field most influential to naturalistic, qualitative research), it is conducted by an outside researcher who applies different treatments or variables to different groups of students to determine the effect of that treatment. (For example, the researcher might administer a pretest of number facts, then ask one teacher to "teach" number facts through flash cards to one group and ask another teacher to "teach" the same to her group using manipulative materials. Afterward, a posttest is administered that produces numerical data to determine how much each group has "learned.") Clearly this type of research is experimental and firmly situated in the positivist paradigm. However, it has one characteristic of naturalistic research—it takes place in the classroom, rather than a laboratory setting.

There are many other combinations of research paradigms, approaches, and methods. How these combinations are made depend greatly on the research question and purpose of a study. These issues will be discussed more fully in later chapters about how to construct your own inquiry.

Different forms of teacher research

Teacher research can take many forms: action research, personal narrative, case study research, ethnography, and others. Although most teacher researchers focus on some aspect of their own work in their own classrooms, some *do* study situations outside their own classroom. Although most teacher research studies rely on qualitative methods, many utilize quantitative methods too. What follows are brief descriptions of some of the different forms that teacher research can take.

Action research ◎ Action research is a study of a situation that is driven by a desire to improve that situation. In an action research study, the researcher investigates an issue, intervenes with something different or new, observes the effects of the action, and reflects on the effects in consideration for further planning (Kemmis, cited in Anderson et al., 1994). Action research often has a cyclical nature. The investigation continually evolves as the action under study is tried, analyzed, implemented, and investigated over and over again. The distinguishing feature of action research is that it is undertaken specifically to improve practice. Other forms of research, in contrast, may result in changed practice, but are not undertaken with that goal in mind.

Teacher researcher Shenaz Carmichael launched an action research project in her first grade classroom when she decided to study her teacher/student reading and writing conferences with the intent of improving them. By studying her documentation of how she conducted her conferences, her records of her students' progress, and her reflections of her practices that she kept in a daily journal, she made changes in the way she scheduled, planned, and carried out literacy conferences in her classroom. Her analysis of what she did and the effects of her actions on her students informed her planning for conferences in the following school year and inspired her to plan additional investigations of other areas of her teaching practice. Shenaz' study provides an in-depth account of the problems and issues she encountered in teaching and how she addressed these problems to make her literacy practices more effective.

Personal narratives ◎ Narrative studies focus on both personal and social aspects of an inquiry. They generally occur in a specific place and take the reader through a sequence of time (Clandinin & Connelly, 2000). In such studies researchers often weave complex, even contradictory stories that may include the past, present, and future. Frequently, the voices of the story's various participants and the personal voice of the researcher are included too. In its telling and retelling, through different voices and in different places, the story's meanings often shift and change. New meanings are constructed and new insights are found as voices are heard and the story unfolds, often in ways that were initially unanticipated (Connelly & Clandinin, 1990).

The narrative form is both a phenomenon and a method (Connelly & Clandinin, 1990). It is based on the premise that understanding is a social process; that truth can be found in the living, telling, retelling, and reliving of stories.

> Stories are powerful research tools. They provide us with a picture of real people in real situations, struggling with real problems. They banish the indifference often generated by samples, treatments, and faceless subjects. They invite us to speculate on what might be changed and with what effect. (Witherell & Noddings, 1991, p. 280)

Stories are recognizable and accessible to most readers. They incorporate lived experiences, sequenced in "real time." They allow us to make comparisons between others' theories, decisions, behaviors, and our own. They lead us to connect to our own experiences, and to imagine new possibilities, directions, or endings for our own lives. Through them we learn something essentially human by understanding an actual life or community as lived (Connelly & Clandinin, 1990).

Besides being a form that addresses human understandings, stories or narratives give new voice and respect to practitioners, whose contribution to the research field has long been undervalued (Lieberman, 1986). Stories are attempts to develop a relationship between theorists and practitioners that honors both—that does not diminish the value of the knowledge of teachers or oversimplify theory, and that does not romanticize teachers or glorify theory.

The story of teacher researcher Yolan Bravo's experience with the death of her two-year-old niece is a personal narrative that examines young children's experiences and understandings of death. In it she simultaneously tells the story of the death's impact on herself and her family; reflects on her own feelings throughout the process of the illness, the death, and the grieving; investigates how young children make sense of this life event; and documents how the educators involved in her niece's life supported her family as they experienced this loss and its accompanying grief. Yolan's completed study offers insights to both her personal experience as well as to how the experience of a young child's death and dying impacts the dying child and the other children and family members involved. A reader of Yolan's study will come away with a heightened sense of awareness of the issues that death and dying arouse, and how a sensitive educator can be of support to those who journey through such an experience.

Case studies ● A case study is an investigation of a particular place or group. It asks a "how" or "why" question about a contemporary situation or set of events (Yin, 1994). It is a holistic and in-depth examination that sheds light on an issue or object. It describes processes and context characteristics that can reveal subtle and unique things. By presenting experience in this way, it has the potential to capitalize on people's natural powers to empathize and understand (Sanders, 1981).

Case studies are not generalizable to populations or universes, as is the intent of experimental studies. They *do* generalize, however, to theoretical propositions (Yin, 1994).

> When explanation, propositional knowledge, and law are the aims of an inquiry, the case study will often be at a disadvantage. When the aims are understanding, extension of experience, and increase in conviction in that which is known, the disadvantage disappears. (Stake, 1978, p. 6)

"Odd Girl Out," a case study by teacher researcher Bridgette Hozumi, examines an all-girl literature circle in her seventh grade classroom. Through a close look at the work of girls in a single-sex literature circle, she gained an understanding of how some of the female students in her class felt about women's roles in society and how gender issues affect them in their homes, communities, and classrooms. In this case study, Bridgette documents how four female students who were placed in a single-sex discussion group transformed from reticent participants, who formerly had deferred to their male classmates, into lively, articulate deep thinkers who actively contributed to the group. As a result, she gained insight to how to create a better environment that is safe and conducive to open expression for all the girls in her class. In this sense, Bridgette's study was not only a case study but an action research project as well.

Ethnography ● Ethnography is the "work of describing and explaining a given culture over time" (Janesick, 1991, p. 101). Utilizing qualitative methods, ethnographies are generally broader and fuller than case studies. What distinguishes them from other research forms is the element of time: Ethnographers stay in a setting for a long period of time to create a holistic portrait of that place. Ethnographies thoroughly examine the relationships, cultures, and systems of the object of their study (Janesick, 1991).

Teacher researcher Allison Schoen's study of multiple intelligences took the form of ethnography. Over the course of an entire school year, she examined different classrooms and teachers in an urban school to learn how the educators there encourage learning and give support to the many different kinds of learners typically found in classrooms. Out of her detailed observations, interviews, and photographic documentation emerged a portrait of school life that revealed the countless little things that adults can do to enhance the learning of diverse learners: how they can talk to children to create an atmosphere of trust and respect, how children's emotional well-being and self-esteem can be supported, how a classroom can be provisioned to encourage active and independent learning, how the content of different disciplines can be presented so that they are accessible to different kinds of learners. An accompanying photographic essay on how children learn through play and everyday activities enriched these understandings and underscored the innate curiosity of young children and the active nature of their learning.

Teachers who are new to research may feel confused by all these different conceptions and choices of research. Don't worry. These issues and ideas will become clearer as you proceed through the chapters of this book and your research project unfolds (see Figure 2–2 for a view of the continuum of research and how the paradigms, approaches, and different research forms fit together). Meanwhile, it is important to remember that there is not one right way to conduct an inquiry. What *is* important is to understand the implications of the

Figure 2–2. Different Research Paradigms and Types of Studies

Positivist paradigm		**Hermaneutic paradigm**	
Experimental approaches		*Naturalistic approaches*	
Experiment	Quasi-Experiment or Process-product research	Survey research	Action research Case study Narrative Ethnography

choices one makes in deciding how to conduct it. A strong researcher can explain why he or she selected to tell a story one way or another, and then can also explain what is lost and what is gained by selecting this approach.

Exercise 1: Identifying different research approaches and methods

Locate different studies about questions that interest you. Analyze them for the following:

- What is the research question or the purpose of the study?
- Identify the data collection methods and data analysis techniques.
- Would you consider the data collection methods to be more quantitative or qualitative?
- Does the study seek to make generalizations, or to find the cause and effect of a particular problem or issue? Would you consider this study to be experimental?
- Or, does the study seek to find "truth" in the particulars? Does it have a more interpretive or naturalistic approach?
- Do you find the study valid and reliable? Why or why not?

Three

Wonderings to Be Done
Finding Your Question

○ ○ ○

*A*s you begin to focus on finding your own research question, topics of interest may easily come to mind. You may have a burning issue you simply cannot wait to explore. However, you may, like many teachers we have known, feel at a loss about what you really want to do. We think that this happens because traditional schooling rarely provides us with opportunities to formulate our own questions. Most of the time we spend in schools focuses on preparing us to answer other peoples' questions. When we finally get the chance to generate our own, we often have difficulty knowing what we want to ask.

It takes a while to begin to understand what research about your own practice can be. Most of us have images of research as being something that is "highbrow" or "academic." Our only images about it come from the experimental model of the scientific community, in which we must prove a hypothesis right or wrong. But research about your practice is different. It is about learning about something that you really care about; about finding out the "how," "what," or "why" of something.

To guide your research you need to develop a research question that will provide a framework for your study and hold it all together. Each element of the study will be related to this overarching question. A research question should not be confused with interview questions. You will not actually be posing this question per se to others in the course of your study. Rather, you will be asking this question to yourself and you will be finding the answer through conducting your study.

Reading examples of teacher research and/or journaling about possible questions that you have about your work can help you come up with a draft of your own question. (For some suggestions, see the list of recommended articles in Appendix 1.) Don't worry if you flounder a bit at first. Eventually you will generate a question that has real meaning and purpose for you. It may be something like one of the following:

> What kinds of teaching strategies can I use to help children get excited about learning?

> How can I create an environment that helps children in my classroom to respect and learn from each other's cultural and ethnic differences?

> What can I do to support literacy development for the students in my class who are not native English speakers?

> How do I engage my students as active partners and support what I know about how children learn in the midst of the testing pressures and curriculum mandates coming from my school and district?

Getting to these questions takes lots of time and exposure to the inquiries and writings of others. As you think about what you want to explore, remember that it doesn't matter if the question you have chosen to pursue has been asked or pursued by someone else before. Remember that "Discovery consists not in seeking new landscapes but in having new eyes" (Marcel Proust).

Awakening your questions

To help you find your research question, take a moment to jot down some of the issues or questions that you have about the work you do. There can be many different types of questions. For example, do you have *questions about improving your teaching practice?* These kinds of questions may arise from a difference between what you intended to do and what actually occurred; from a routine that did not work, a conflict, a desire to try something new, a concern about a child's progress. They might look something like these: How can I maintain discipline in my classroom? How can I make better use of my reading/writing conferences with students? How can I do more peer work? How can I incorporate more active learning or project-based work into the schedule of my day?

Or, do you have *questions about* your *relations with other adults in the school environment?* How can I develop better home/school partnerships? How can I work more effectively with my co-teacher in our inclusion classroom? How can I help the other teachers in my childcare center to discipline children more appropriately?

Do you have *questions about your school's practices or policies?* What is the impact of a uniform policy on the children in the school? What are the challenges presented by the new reading curriculum? How do pressures from high-stakes tests affect teachers and children in my school?

Or, finally, do you have *questions about learning or growth in other parts of your life outside the school context?* Are you struggling with how to help your own personal child or a child in your classroom deal with a divorce, a health crisis, or a death? Do you have torn loyalties between being a stay-at-home or a working parent?

All these questions are grist for inquiry. You can study them as you live your life. And because the purpose of such questions is to find out the deep meaning or impact of an issue directly related to you, one could argue that you are best situated to study them because your vantage point as a teacher in a classroom or a person living your life provides a unique perspective that outsiders can never hope to obtain.

This kind of research is different from research that is conducted by people outside of classrooms using large-scale data sets or questionnaires. Although it may look at the same issues that large-scale research does, it does so from a different perspective. Although large-scale research is conducted to provide important information about trends or about the broad impact of issues on large groups, your own inquiry research aims to enrich and deepen understandings that this other research, because of its very nature, cannot yield. Inquiry research is thus aimed at giving a full and thorough examination of particulars. And through the examination of particulars, it can lead to recognition of other such particulars in new and foreign contexts, and thus add to existing experiences and understandings (Merriam, 1988).

Framing your question

As you think about the kinds of questions you may have, it is important to note two distinguishing characteristics of the kinds of questions best suited for teacher inquiry research. The first thing to take note of is the way that inquiry questions are framed. Unlike questions developed for experimental research, inquiry questions are not generated as a hypothesis that leads to a proof or disproof. They do not ask questions that can be answered with a simple yes or no. Rather, they are framed to probe into an issue; to understand better the meaning and nature of a particular condition, to yield a "thick" description (Geertz, 1973; Merryfield, 1990; Patton, 1990) of the "how" or "what" or "why" of a situation. Inquiry questions seek in-depth answers or explanations that get beneath the surface of an experience.

The second important characteristic of inquiry-oriented questions for teacher research is that they are particular, not universal. They examine the impact of the issue directly on you. The kind of research on which we focus in this book is not meant to examine issues from a mega-analysis. As teachers, we are not in the best position to address definitively how an issue impacts everywhere. For example, questions such as how race and class impact student achievement or why students of color are disproportionately represented in special education require statistical analyses of data sets across large groups of students. These are important questions, but they are not ones that we are best situated to research in this way. However, we *are* best equipped to examine how these questions play out in the particulars of our classrooms or our schools. We *can* design a study that will allow us to examine the factors that led the students in our special education classroom to be referred. Or we *can* look at the nature of the support that successful students from underresourced communities receive from their families (see Exercise 1 at the end of the chapter).

Getting started

So, here is a suggestion for how to get started generating your question: Keep a journal over the next week or two of what happens in your classroom and life. Jot down the things that excite you, bother you, and/or interest you. Note your wonderings, your puzzlements, and your queries. At the end of the week, review and reflect on your writings to identify issues you might want to examine in greater depth. Then generate a list of questions from these issues and select one that you really care about (see Exercise 2 at the end of this chapter).

You may not be settled on a question by the end of the week. You may not have found a question that is appealing to you. You may find that you are still torn between several issues you find to be of interest. You may feel that you need more information about an issue to make a commitment about your question. Or, you may be confused about exactly how to frame your question. If any of these is the case for you, don't worry. All learning takes time. You may simply need more time. (Remember this—and the uncertainty you feel now—when you are working with your own students.)

Depending on which of these issues is holding you up, try either (1) journaling for a longer period of time to find a truly burning issue, (2) reading what others have had to say about the issue that interests you (see Chapter 4), or (3) sharing your question with a friend or colleague for help in framing your question. As you frame your possible question, ask yourself the following: Is your question in an inquiry mode? (Is it a "what," "how," or "why" question)? Note, however, that all "how," "what," or "why" questions are not suited for teacher inquiry. For instance, "why" questions can be tricky in that they sometimes require the researcher to come up with a simple solution to a complex question. Is your question framed in a way that is personalized to your situation? Can you pursue it in the context of your life? Do you already know the answer to your question? If so, keep playing with your question to make it more open-ended. Is this question meaningful to you in your life as a teacher? (See Exercise 3 at the end of the chapter.)

Developing subquestions

To help make your question more manageable, the next step you will want to take is to develop subquestions for it. Subquestions help define what you are going to examine within the context of your question. The subquestions will serve as a guide for your inquiry, helping you to decide what tools to use for your study and aiding your analysis of the information you collect. (This will be explained more in subsequent chapters.) For now, though, you need to think about what aspects of your question or issue you want to pursue.

For example, if your question is about how play supports young children's learning, your subquestions might be the following: How does play support cognitive development? How does play support social/emotional development? How does play support physical development? You might even want to add: How can I explain the benefits of play to the families of the children in my class? Remember, each of the subquestions should be connected to your big question. Each subquestion is one piece of the bigger question. The subquestions help to manage the exploration of the main question.

Questions evolve

Sometimes questions evolve through a study and don't get formulated fully until the study is well underway. This open-endedness is uncomfortable for some people who just want to select a question and subquestions and be done with this phase of the process. In many cases, however, when questions evolve, it is often because the inquirer has learned more about his or her topic and needs to refine the question to reflect this new knowledge. The study by teacher researcher Michael Zimski is an example of this. He began with the question: How do I manage negative behaviors in the classroom? As he read various articles and books on discipline and tried out suggested practices in his classroom, he began to realize that the question he needed to explore was of quite a different nature. Not until he reached the conclusion of his study did he come to understand that his real question was about "How do I create community in the classroom?"

Originally I was looking for ideas that would help me address certain types of negative classroom behavior. In essence, I was searching for ways to react to situations rather than to prevent them. The more I learned from my readings and experiences, the more I came to see that most of my questions were the wrong ones to ask to obtain the information that I really wanted to know. Creating community in the classroom, I concluded, is the key to answering my original research question. The most effective way to manage a group of students is to create a safe, nurturing community where they can learn and grow.

Another teacher researcher, Juliana Sage, first formulated her research question as: What tests can I use to evaluate children's learning? Through her readings she came to see a broader view of evaluation and eventually changed her question to: What forms of evidence can I collect to identify children's strengths and inform my teaching? She explains:

Through my study I came to a new understanding of what assessment truly is. I had started out thinking that assessment was a test you gave to a student, graded it, and taught him what s/he did not know. Yes, I still believe that assessment is the acquiring and analyzing of information to further my children's learning, but now I believe its purpose is to identify students' strengths not just their weaknesses. I also learned that assessment should be tailored to the individual child, take many forms, include observation and record keeping, and be antibiased.

Teacher researcher Michelle Gill changed her question many times throughout the course of her study. Frustrated with a parent of a child in her class whom Michelle believed needed to be referred to special education, she first asked: How do I work with parents who are in denial of their children's special needs? As she learned, through her readings, more about issues related to special needs, she changed her question to: How can I work with parents to understand their children with special needs? Finally, as she pursued this question and began to apply her new-found understandings, Michelle changed her perspective on the issue and reshaped her question once again to: How can I work together with a parent of a special needs child to support the child better? This progression in the question's form and tone reflects the progression of Michelle's learning. She began to acquire a more complex perspective on special needs, understand the benefits of an inclusion approach for the education of children with special needs, gain appreciation and empathy for parents of children with special needs, and recognize the importance of home–school partnerships. The story of Michelle's changing research question is, in fact, the story of her growth as a teacher, as she explains:

> Interviewing the child's mother was a turning point for me as an educator because I had some false perceptions of her and her understanding of her child. Through my study I learned that, in fact, she was very aware of who her child is, what his abilities are, and that she indeed held very high expectations for his development and his success as a learner.

To guide you as you develop the subquestions for your big question, try posing the following questions to yourself: Is each subquestion connected to my big question? Is each subquestion a component of my bigger question? Will the subquestion help to manage the exploration of my main question? If you have answered yes to these, you have the foundation for your inquiry (see Exercise 4 at the end of the chapter).

Explaining what you plan to do in your study
Now that you have settled on a question and formulated your subquestions, think about exactly what you want to do in your study to pursue the answers to your questions.

Do you want to explore your question by *reading about strategies for how to do something and then trying out those strategies in your classroom?* For example, if your study is about how to discipline, do you want to read about classroom management, try out the techniques you have learned, and then document what happens when you use them?

Or do you want to explore your question by *examining how a theory plays out in the classroom and how you best can apply that theory to practice?* For example, if your question is about multiple intelligences, do you want to test what you have read about in the theory by looking for ways that your teaching and your classroom environment support children's multiple intelligences? Or, if your question is about how play can support children's development, do you want to examine the play of the children in your classroom and analyze what goes on in relation to different learning theories?

Do you want to investigate a phenomenon and reflect on its implications for your teaching? For example, if your question is about parent involvement, do you want to examine how well you involve parents in the educational life of your classroom? Or, if your question is about gender differences, do you want to look at the impact that gender has on how children interact in literature groups?

Or *do you want to pursue your question through an intensive study of a child in your classroom?* For example, if your question is about reading difficulties, do you want to examine these in one child? As Michelle's story demonstrates, we teachers often bring our own prejudices or lack of knowledge to how we perceive and then interact with children in our classrooms. Studying a particular child can help us see the child in a different light; can reveal the child's strengths and interests, as well as help us gain insight to the nuances of his/her areas of vulnerability. An in-depth look at one child through the systematic gathering of evidence yields understandings about growth and development that can be applicable to all children. This child study approach to research began in the early 1900s and has been put to use contemporarily in the work of Cohen et al. (1996), Carini (1987), Almy & Genishi (1979), and others.

Now that you have a sense of different ways to pursue your question, take a moment to clarify, for yourself and for those with whom you will share your study, what you think you want to do. The details concerning "who," "what," and "how" can be worked out later (see Chapter 5 on how to develop your research design). Right now it is enough for you to have a general idea of where you want to go (see Exercise 5 at the end of the chapter).

Clarifying the context and background of your question
Finally, for this first stage of your project, make sure you are clear about why you want to pursue your study. What leads you to it and why? Write a few paragraphs to yourself (and others) about this, explaining your purpose for this study and why and how your question arose. This will help

you, as well as those with whom you will share your work, to understand better exactly what you are trying to do.

Also in this section, think about the perspective and/or biases you have that might impact how you approach your study. Is your study of dual-language classrooms coming as a result of your positive or negative experiences with such programs? Is your exploration of teachers' feelings about balanced literacy influenced by your like or dislike of its approaches? Is your examination of how to incorporate investigations of the natural world into your curriculum instigated from your own love or fearfulness of science? It is okay to bring biases to your inquiry—because everyone has them, after all—as long as you openly admit them and continually reflect on how they might affect what you conclude. As discussed in the previous chapter, feelings and ideas and personal experiences influence everything that we do. We cannot completely extricate ourselves from them. All we can ask of ourselves is to be transparent about what we think and how our thinking may affect what we see (see Exercise 6 at the end of the chapter).

When you have completed these steps, you will have completed the initial part of your inquiry: your overarching question, your subquestions, what you plan to approach the investigation of your question, your explanation of the context and background of your study, and the perspective/biases that you bring to it.

Here are a few examples excerpted from the studies of some teacher researchers we know. Shenaz Carmichael and Natalie McCabe wrote these descriptions before they conducted their study. Bridgette's piece was revised after she completed her investigation.

Shenaz' Study

The question I chose to do my research on is: How can I make my reading and writing conferences more effective? There are four subquestions that I plan to explore to help me with this project:

1. How do you manage conferences in a Reading and Writing Workshop?

2. What do you do in a reading–writing conference?

3. What do you do with the information you gain from conferring with students in a Reading and Writing Workshop?

4. How does conferring with students help them become better readers and writers?

What I plan to do ◦ I plan on reading literature on conferencing and applying it to my classroom. The staff developer in my school has also agreed to help me with my conferencing. Also, I plan on using my own experiences and my conferencing notes.

Context/background for my question ◦ I chose the topic because it is something that I have been concerned about for a few years now. My first year [of teaching] I did not do much conferencing, but as the years went on I began to conference much more. However, I think that I definitely need to fine-tune my conferencing. I tend to spend too much time with one student and never seem to stick to my conferencing schedule. As a result, I do not see my students as often as I should.

I believe that I am trying to do too much during each conference and that is why they last as long as they do. When I finish with my conference, I put my notes in my binder and never look at them again until parent–teacher conferences. I am hoping that doing a research paper on this topic will help me become better at conferencing and, in turn, will help me to become a better teacher to my students this year and the years to come.

Natalie's Study

Research question ◦ The purpose of this study is how to explore how I can best support the autonomy of my students through play in learning centers. I hope to discover how play in centers can support a child's social, behavioral, physical, and academic development.

◦ *Subquestions*

How are children their own teachers in learning centers?

How does play in centers impact children's development?

How can my anecdotals and observations of students at centers drive my teaching?

How do children extend what they learn in mini lessons to their play?

What I plan to do ○ For the purpose of this study, I will observe conversations, actions, interactions, reactions, behavioral patterns, and the overall climate of the environment in learning centers. I will observe and document behaviors and the use of materials and manipulatives in centers.

Context/background ○ I worked for one year in a "Success for All" mandated curriculum school. We spent the first half of this year "phasing out" "Success for All" and beginning implementation of a balanced literacy approach. The role of centers in my classroom has changed dramatically during the process. Last year, centers were theme based and task oriented. There was a certain block of time at the end of the day for centers. However, I was always intrigued by how children made their greatest and most rewarding discoveries independent of the assigned tasks. This year, beginning in January, my classroom became a balanced literacy environment. Learning centers are integrated throughout the day during Readers and Writers Workshops. The center activities and tasks are based on the needs of the children. I am able to design activities based on observations and anecdotals, and work in small groups. However, I am exploring a time for children to have free play in my classroom.

I hope that with this growing freedom from obligatory tasks and activities, I will be able to plan and create my lessons from the play I see in centers. I hope that a methodology for assessment-driven instruction for increasingly independent learners will result from this study. I know my bias is on the end of the spectrum opposite task orientation, and as such I see the children as drivers in the course of their learning.

Bridgette's Study

As a middle school teacher in a New York City public school, this has been a year of great change and uncertainty. With a huge curricular overhaul, it has become the responsibility of the teacher to wade through mountains of material, many times contradictory, to find the right material for his or her students within the prescribed framework of balanced literacy and the workshop model.

One of the structures within the balanced literacy workshop framework is literature circles—peer-led discussions of literature.

These take place within the group work or independent work time within the reading workshop. At first mention of these literature circles, while attending professional development workshops last summer, I was excited at the prospect of more cooperative learning in the literacy classroom. During the previous year, cooperative learning was very successful in my literacy classes, alleviating some of the many discipline issues that were arising as a first-year teacher, engaging the children's interest, and taking pressure off me to be the sole expert in the classroom. I was able to defer to the children's text connections and facilitate rather than lecture.

Feeling enthused about the new system I would be setting up in my current seventh grade literacy class, I went home to review my lesson plans and postlesson notes from last year. As I looked through my materials, my memories of my wonderful cooperative learning experiences began to give way to the reality of what had actually happened in my lessons. There were students who could not remain on task, who made inappropriate remarks while seemingly outside the gaze of the teacher, and, most memorably, there was Janine. Janine was a 12-year-old girl in my class who was very motivated when working individually or with her friend, Teresita, the only other girl in my predominantly male class, but she completely shut down when put into a group situation. I recalled, as I reread my notes, how many different combinations I had tried with Janine in different mixes of children, but to no avail. She would not participate when in a small-group situation. Janine also expressed to me on several occasions her loathing of group work and pleaded to be able to work alone or solely with Teresita.

As this year progressed, I had noticed a similar situation arising with some girls in my evenly gender-divided seventh grade literacy class. Although many look forward to group work when given the choice to work only with girlfriends, they shy away from grouped situations in which they must function in a male–female group. This is a phenomenon that I have, until recently, taken for granted as a normal and acceptable choice. However, thinking back to Janine's experiences last year in my literacy classes, it seems unfair to place students, particularly female students, in a situation that does not encourage or allow for high achievement or success.

Thus, when I came across a journal article by Dillow et al. (1994, p. 48) that asked, "Do female students benefit from and achieve at higher levels under certain cooperative learning conditions?" I was intrigued. Their research question thus put my wonderings into words and led me to my research question. It was the female students' perspective of group work in the literacy classroom, particularly literature circles, of which I wanted to gain a greater understanding in my action research project. Through a closer look at how girls worked in single-sex literature circles, I hoped to gain a greater understanding of how best to incorporate literature circles to create an environment that is safe and conducive to open expression to females who often feel marginalized in literacy class.

I began observing the girls' literature circles once a week, documenting their conversations and book talks. In addition, after and during each literature circle we would discuss open-ended questions in a focus-group format. I listened as the girls asked deep, relevant questions of one another and themselves, and watched as they began to deconstruct their world through literature and academic discussion. These observations helped me to answer my research question:

> Do female students benefit from and achieve at higher levels under single-sex conditions in literature circles?

And my subquestions:

> Does book choice greatly impact the relevance of discussions in an all-girl literature circle?

> Do girls feel more comfortable in orally responding to literature in an all-girl literature circle?

> Do the adjustments that I may feel necessary to help my female students succeed still fit under the umbrella of the workshop model and balanced literacy curriculum?

Each of these descriptions of research has an open-ended question or statement of the research issue, followed by subquestions that help clarify how the researcher is interpreting her question and how she intends to investigate the larger question. Each teacher's description also offers a clear explanation of how she came to the question from her own context, and why the question is important to her.

Research with children: Helping children find their questions
You can help your students conduct their own inquiries in much the same way as the process that has just been described for teachers. However,

children will generally not be studying themselves in the same way we have described examining our own practice. Children *can* use the inquiry process, however, to explore issues or topics of interest to them. These explorations can be done through whole-class or individual investigations.

Group studies

A classroomwide or group study that is based on children's questions is a great way not only to model inquiry in your classroom, but to help students actively shape their learning experiences. A group study of an issue or topic can develop in many different ways. It can emerge from questions related to the mandated curriculum of your district or state, it can evolve from a trip or activity experienced by the group, it can arise from a question or issue that was discussed at a class meeting, or it can grow out of classroom disagreements, issues, or questions that come up during the school day.

Teacher researcher Ryan Flessner developed a group study with his fourth graders based on a phenomenon he repeatedly saw taking place during literature circle time. Although he consistently modeled ways to raise questions and respond to each other, he was disturbed that his students were not truly engaging in "accountable talk" (Resnick, 2001). They seemed to be trying to win his approval rather than genuinely involving themselves in their conversations about books. He raised this issue with his students and asked them if he could videotape them having conversations in their literature groups. After this was done, the students and he viewed the videotape together, critiqued what they saw, and then developed their own list of criteria of what makes a good conversation about literature. They created an evaluation form for the criteria and then tried the literature circles several more times. After each conversation, they discussed the process and reevaluated how they had done. Ryan then videotaped the literature circles again, and followed the taping with a class discussion about what changes they had seen. They continued this process in a spiraling format (Bruner, 1960), making changes, then evaluating the changes, and following with more plans for more improvements over time.

Not only did the literature circle strategy begin to work better in his classroom, but Ryan was also able both to model and provide opportunities for his students to problem solve, systematically conduct research, develop criteria, and analyze data over time. Most important, through this group research project, Ryan sent a message to his students conveying his trust in their judgments and his belief that genuine involvement in learning, not simply obedience to his authority, is of the highest value in their classroom.

Another example of how a group study can evolve is the investigation of students' cultures and backgrounds that was done in Sasha Wilson's second/third grade class. The impetus for the study was a racial slur made by one child to another during recess that Sasha just happened to overhear. He used this event as the focus of a class meeting in which the children raised issues and questions about their different skin colors, languages, cultures, and family backgrounds. Subsequently they spent many weeks investigating their differences. They searched for information from the Internet and other printed information, from trips, and from interviews with each other's family members. They cooked, wrote poetry, made self-portraits, and, finally, wrote reports about different aspects of the cultural mosaic that they came to value in their classroom community.

Individual investigations

In addition to whole-group studies, individual research projects can also help children develop as learners. Children's individual inquiries can emerge from units you are covering in class, from individual books the children are reading, or from the choices of your students. As you may have experienced yourself, getting in touch with your genuine interests is not always easy. You may need to help the children in your class figure out what they want to investigate. They may need help identifying what they are curious about, what matters to them, or what they want to learn. When given the opportunity and some practice, however, we predict you will find that most children have their own ideas about what subjects they want to explore.

To introduce children to individual investigations, invite them to make a list of things they are interested in or want to know more about. After they generate this list, they will need to choose one topic from it that they want to explore. Make sure to give them adequate time to work on doing this (Falk & Margolin, 2005).

When the children have selected an individual or class topic, ask them to write about it in the same way that you articulated the background and context for your own inquiry. You can guide them by asking them why they chose it, what they already know about it, and what else they would like to learn about it (New York City Writing Project, 1982).

Collect the questions and the background statements, review them, and provide feedback to each child. Make sure your comments are supportive and educative; in other words, first find something positive about which to comment, then ask questions that push for clarification or elaboration, or that probe toward deeper understanding.

Framing the question

With children, too, brainstormed topics must be turned into researchable questions. Some students have difficulty understanding how to do this. They may need help learning how to distinguish questions that can be answered with a simple fact from questions that involve analysis and interpretation. Or they may not understand the difference between questions that yield one-word answers from questions that lead to other significant questions. Some may not know how to explore the unfamiliar or how to delve deeply into a subject.

To address any of these issues, it is a good idea to call the class together to have a "mini lesson" about how to frame a question. In this lesson you can help the children understand how different ways of framing questions can produce different kinds of answers. Make sure to present the difference between questions that begin with "how," "what," or "why" and questions that lead to yes or no answers. Go over several examples before sending the children off to settle on and frame their own question. After they make their final choice, a nice extension of this work is to have them write their question on a paper strip, decorate it, and post it on the classroom walls (Falk & Margolin, 2005).

Next, the children will need help learning how to "unpack" their questions into subquestions that will help them further define and investigate their topics. Guide them with the same type of queries that you posed to yourself when you generated your own subquestions. Make sure that their subquestions are related to their big question and offer them a structure for how to proceed in their study. As they set about writing these subquestions, allow them to work independently and be available to give them help.

As with the earlier examples of teacher inquiries, some children may not know enough about the topic they want to investigate to know what kind of questions to ask. They may need to look for information first before they can generate the little questions. If so, allow them to explore some of the literature on their topics before proceeding to write their subquestions.

Exercise 1: Framing your question

Take a topic or issue and turn it into a research question. How would you ask the question if you were going to design an experimental study around it? How would you ask the question if you were going to design an inquiry study around it?

Exercise 2: Selecting your question

To help you get started with developing research questions

- Keep a journal over the next week or two of the happenings in your classroom and life (Many teachers find it helpful to carry a small notebook in their pocket to take quick notes during the day as ideas come to them.)

- Jot down the things that excite you, bother you, and/or interest you

- Note your wonderings, your puzzlements, and/or your queries

- At the end of the week, review and reflect on your writings to identify issues you might want to examine in more depth

- Then generate a list of questions from these issues and select one that you really care about

Exercise 3: Questions to ask yourself about your question

- Is your question framed clearly?

- Is your question in an inquiry mode? (Is it a "what," "how," or "why" question?)

- Is your question framed in a way that is personalized to your situation?

- Is your question researchable in the context of your life?

- Is your question "loaded"? In other words, are your assumptions part of the question?

- Do you already know the answer to your question? If so, keep playing with your question to make it more open-ended.

- Does your question pass the "so what" test? Is this question meaningful to you in your life as a teacher? Will it interest other teachers?

Exercise 4: Questions to ask yourself about your subquestions

- Is each subquestion connected to your big question?
- Is each subquestion framed in an open-ended way?
- Will the subquestions help to manage the exploration of your main question?

Exercise 5: Deciding on what you plan to do in your study

How do you want to approach the pursuit of your question?

- Do you want to read about strategies for how to do something and then try out those strategies in your classroom?
- Do you want to examine how a theory plays out in the classroom and how you best can apply that theory to practice?
- Do you want to investigate a phenomenon and reflect on its implications for your teaching?
- Do you want to pursue your question through an intensive study of a child in your classroom?

Exercise 6: Clarifying the context and background of your question

- How did you come to your question?
- Why do you want to pursue it?
- What perspectives and/or biases might you have that will impact how you approach your question?

Exercise 7: Helping children generate questions

To facilitate the development of questions in your classroom, reflect on the following:

- Are there opportunities in your class for children to share their ideas?
- Is there space during the school day for children's interests, desires, or questions to arise?

- If not, how can you make room in your busy school day for children to have these kinds of experiences?

- Jot down your answers and discuss them with a colleague.

Exercise 8: Developing a research question and subquestion with children

You can use the process outlined in the following student worksheet to help children develop questions for inquiry. Make sure to adapt this worksheet to the age of your students, the scope of the projects you want to launch, and other contextual issues. Before asking students to complete this, make sure that you introduce and explain how to do each step of the process, model how to proceed, and follow up with mini lessons as needed.

Worksheet for Developing Inquiry Questions

Choose a topic

      Brainstorm a list of topics you want to explore.

      Which of these topics are more compelling or interesting to you?

Choose one topic to pursue

Write about why you chose that topic, what you already know about it, and what you want to learn about it.

Frame your research question

Write your big research question:

      Is it framed in an open-ended way or is it a question with a yes or no answer?

      Is it researchable?

Creating subquestions

Brainstorm six (or more) possible subquestions to your big questions:

    1.   4.

    2.   5.

    3.   6.

Review your subquestions and cross out the questions that do not seem to be working.

      Do they break down the big question into smaller ideas, or are they moving you in a new direction?

      Will you be able to find out answers to each of these questions?

      Are the questions open-ended or are they questions with yes or no answers?

Write your three subquestions and then discuss them with a partner:

    1.

    2.

    3.

Standing on the Shoulders
of Those Who Came Before

○ ○ ○

*T*o situate your question in a larger framework and to place it in the context of existing knowledge, you need to conduct a review of the literature. This type of review will apprise you of the kinds of studies that have already been done on your topic and what has been learned about it and other related issues.

You might approach a review of the literature for your topic from several angles. You might turn to the literature because you don't really know what you want to study but know the topic in which you are interested. By reviewing the literature that exists, you learn more about the topic, which should help you more easily develop and shape the question you want to explore.

Or, you may be clear about your question, but need more ideas about how to approach your study. Examining the literature will expose you to the different ways that others have explored this topic. For example, you may want to do a study that confirms or disproves what someone else has found, or you might want to model your study on the methods used by someone else. From reading the work of others, you might get ideas for how to organize your study, what methods to use, what questions to ask, or how to write up your findings. Or, after reading about the topic that is of interest to you, you might even find that what you want to do has not been done before! This was the case for Carol Gilligan, the well-known gender theorist, who, when reviewing the literature on moral development, was surprised to find that the only studies on this topic were done with boys. There was a gap in the literature and she decided to fill it (Gilligan, 1982). Thus began a whole new field. It is possible that the same could happen to you!

Reviewing the literature about your area of interest could even lead you to rephrase or reframe your question. Remember the story in Chapter 3 of how Michael transformed his research question? After he read about discipline, his area of interest, he realized that the questions he was focusing on were all wrong. Or think back to Juliana's revelation about her question (also in Chapter 3). After reading about assessment, she came to understand that assessment meant much more than simply test scores.

After you read about your topic, you might find that you agree or disagree with some of the authors. Some things you have read might not make sense to you. You might find that you have ideas about how a study could have been done differently. Or you might discover that there are different perspectives on the same issue. You may need to compare and contrast the studies so that you eventually can get a better sense of where you stand on the question in relation to the approach of others. Your exploration of what others have written can help you understand different perspectives about or approaches to your topic. You can use these understandings to adopt your own perspective on your question. For example, as you read about literacy learning you will see that the subject is approached from widely different perspectives—from a focus on sequentially learning discreet skills before emphasizing comprehension, to a focus on learning skills in the context of experiences with an early emphasis on meaning. As you read about these differing perspectives, you will get a clearer sense of your own views, what perspective you want to take, and how you want to approach your study. This will help you figure out where you and your study fit within the larger debates (see Exercise 4 at the end of the chapter).

It is often useful to begin a search by seeing if studies like yours have been conducted previously. For some topics there will be ample studies available. For instance, if you are exploring methodologies for teaching first graders to read, you will most likely find many studies that have been conducted on the topic. Do not worry if you find a study that looks very similar to the one you are planning to do. This is a sign of how significant this topic is to many people. The fact that it is similar can be helpful in several ways. It can help you because you can use the similar study to figure out what you want to do differently or the same in yours. Or, it can be helpful to others that you are doing a similar study in that your study could add more or even new information to the literature. In addition, the understandings you gain from exploring how the issue in which you are interested plays out in your unique context could turn out to be helpful to others who are in similar settings.

Some research topics may not have very much, or even any, literature to consult. If this is the case for you, you may need to examine several different literature areas to piece together the background information that you need. For instance, teacher researcher Jumel Carlos created a study on the role of ebonics in the editing part of the writing process with his sixth grade students. He was unable to find a study exactly like his own. Therefore, he looked across different areas of research for his literature review. He read studies about ebonics, about editing, and about the writing process with sixth grade students. After reading research from these different areas, Jumel was able to create a review of literature that was informative to his work.

As you can see, the different parts of the inquiry process are interconnected. Sometimes the steps are sequential; sometimes they are not. Generally, they interweave and intermix. You might develop your question first, then learn what others have said about it. Or you might have a general interest that you are unable to form into a question until you learn about what others have learned. In either case, the process usually involves several iterations of questioning, learning, questioning. A literature review, by exploring others' work, gives you a foundation on which to move forward.

Beginning your investigation

Where do you go to find books, periodical or newspaper articles, statistical information, or websites about your topic of interest? You can search the Internet, library resources, or consult experts in the field.

Using the Internet ○ The Internet has search engines that will hunt for documents in the World Wide Web. Some are advertisement free, such as *www.google.com* and *www.northernlight.com*. Other search engines have commercials, such as *www.askjeeves.com, www.altavista.com, www.excite.com, www.msn.com, www.yahoo.com, www.webcrawler.com, www.hotpot.com*, and *www.refdesk.com*. There are even search engines for specific topics. Among the educational search engines are *www.askeric.org, www.eric.net*, and *www.worldwidelearn.com*. And finally, there are search engines that search several search engines at one time, such as *www.dogpile.com*.

If you are looking for statistical information, there are Internet sites devoted exclusively to this. Among them are

Statistical Abstract of the United States: *www.census.gov/state_abstract*

FirstGov: *www.firstgov.gov*

Google Uncle Sam: *www.google.com/unclesam*

Factfinder: *factfinder.census.gov*

The White House: *www.whitehouse.gov/fsbr/esbr.html*

STAT-USA Internet: *www.stat-usa.gov*

Regardless of the vehicle you are searching, use your research question or, if you don't have that yet, a statement of your investigating interest as a guide to finding information. Try to tease out two or three concepts connected to your topic. For example, let's use the question: What teaching strategies can support heterogeneous grouping in the primary grades? The key words or concepts in this sentence are

Concept 1	Concept 2	Concept 3
teaching strategies	heterogeneous grouping	primary grades

Because these concepts or key words have more than one word, when using them for a search, put parentheses around the whole phrase. Otherwise, the search engine will give you all the information it can find for each separate word. If you put an *and* in between the phrases when doing a search, the search engine will find you articles, books, or other information that simultaneously address all three concepts.

Concept 1		Concept 2		Concept 3
(teaching strategies)	and	(heterogeneous grouping)	and	(primary grades)

To increase the chances of finding information about these concepts, you can also provide the search engine with synonyms (get these from a thesaurus) of your concepts, using the word *or.*

Concept 1		Concept 2		Concept 3
(teaching strategies)	and	(heterogeneous grouping)	and	(primary grades)

or	or	or
(teaching practices)	(mixed-ability grouping)	(early childhood education)
or	or	or
(teaching methods)	(nontracked classes)	(young children's learning)

The rule to remember is that the word *or* broadens your search; the word *and* narrows your search. If you want to narrow your search further, you can use the word *not* to eliminate an unwanted combination, as in Concept 3:

Concept 3

(primary grades) or (early childhood education) not
(elementary education)

When you perform your search and look at the results, you might decide that you need to refine or modify the search further. If you have too few references, go back to the search screen and add or change descriptors or key words. If you have too much information that does not relate to your topic, you can also limit your search by defining what language, date, or publication type you want to receive (see Exercise 1 at the end of the chapter).

Make sure to save your search results. For more information about how to conduct Internet searches, consult websites that offer thorough guides, such as *http://webquest.sdsu.edu/searching/fournets.htm* or *noodletools.com.*

The Internet has grown rapidly during the last decade. In 1993 there were only something like fourteen websites. Today there are many millions! It is likely that you will find information from a variety of sources. Among the multitude of resources are sites developed by individuals, government agencies, profit and nonprofit organizations, magazines, and professional journals. Because anyone can post information on an Internet site, it is very important to evaluate critically the information that you find. Who posted it? What evidence is provided to support the information that is presented? Although critical evaluation of *anything* that you read is always important, the proliferation of information on the Internet has made it especially critical to evaluate carefully.

One way to help distinguish the kind of information offered at different sites is by the ending of the URL (the address of the site). Anything that ends in "edu" is from an educational institution—universities and/or school systems. Anything that ends in "org" is from a group or organization. An ending of "com" usually signals that it is a commercial site. "net" means a network, "gov" is a government site, and "mil" is a site sponsored by the military. These clues can help a little to let you know where the information is coming from, but you still must always be vigilant. Look for information that is presented with references. Beware of sloganeering or partisan arguments. Know that there are sites that try to fool readers by presenting themselves one way when in reality they are putting forth an opposite view. For example, in a Google search for Martin Luther King, a website turns up what, at first glance, appears to be about MLK but in reality is a site that offers a white supremacist view of MLK and his work (Gersh, 2004).

To check out the credibility of the information on a new website, first check to see who the author is. If the author is one person, check to see if that person is reputable by looking for any listed credentials. If the author is an organization, check it out in the *Encyclopedia of Associations* in your library. If an address or e-mail address is given, you might want to use it to investigate further.

Another thing you want to know about a website is the country or state that the site comes from. This will help you put the information that you find there in a context. Having a context will also help you find out how objective the website is. Knowing its purpose—to inform you, convince you of a point of view, sell you a product or service, amuse or entertain you—will help you discern whether the information you are presented with is worthy of your attention. Knowing how current the website's content is will also add to your ability to determine credibility. Check to see when the website was last updated.

To get a sense of how useful the website will be to you, make sure you find out who its intended audience is. You want a site that is appropriate for you or your students' age and reading level. And lastly, check out how the website is organized. A useful website will be well designed (i.e., organized logically and easy to navigate) (Gersh, 2004) (see Exercise 2 at the end of the chapter).

There are many Internet sites that offer criteria and processes for evaluating websites. Some even provide examples and exercises. (For a list of some sites to consult, see Appendix 2.)

Searching for books and periodicals   Although the Internet is dominant in our current "information age," books and periodicals still remain valuable sources of knowledge and information. However, with the increasing technological transformation of libraries, you can search for books and periodicals in much the same way as you search the Internet—by identifying key words or concepts from a statement about your research topic as described earlier. Remember always to consult your librarian to find out the details of how to do this in the library you use. Most libraries now purchase on-line databases that include hundreds of journal sources. Library searches can even be conducted in many libraries from your home computer with the use of a password or identification number, if your school or institution subscribes. Often, you can even download the full text of a journal from home.

Professional educational journals are most often your best bet in finding trustworthy materials. They generally are made up mostly of articles that are based on research and have been reviewed anonymously by an editorial board of professionals in the appropriate field. (This is different from the types of articles and ways of selecting them used by magazines. Magazines are generally pitched to a specific audience and typically contain articles selected or invited by an editor that feature reporting, essays, or opinions, as opposed to systematic research.) Although professional journals may present ideas with which you agree or disagree, you can at least be sure that what you are reading in them is based on evidence that has been reviewed by several readers and then approved by an editorial board. However, even when reading an article in a journal, you must still maintain your critical eye. What journals choose to publish are also influenced by the varying perspectives of the different readers and editorial boards. Their own educational philosophies, political leanings, and/or theoretical frameworks cannot help but affect their decisions to accept or reject potential manuscripts. Therefore, it is still important when reading any information always to ask yourself such questions as: Who is saying this? From what perspective? Do I agree or disagree?

An effective way to find interesting informational sources is to consult the reference lists in other books or articles you have read. One article will lead you to others, which can lead you to countless others.

Ask an expert ◉ Interviewing an individual who is knowledgeable about your topic can be an effective way to get information. Find out the important people in your field and make appointments to talk to them. Formulate your questions in advance. Take notes but, if you can, audiotape the conversation so that you do not miss any important details.

Citing references

At the end of your literature review, you will need to provide a list of all the sources you consulted or quoted to prepare it. You need to do this for several reasons:

1. You want to know who said what and how to find this information again.

2. You want to alert others to the information you have found and they will need the reference information to find it.

3. You want to credit others for their ideas or, if you use their words (in your writing or talking), you must acknowledge them with quotes and cited information.

Although there are several reference format styles, the one generally used in the field of education is the American Psychological Association (APA) style. This style lists all references at the end of your writing, *and* credits (within the body of the writing) any author whose ideas or words you have used. How to do these references is explained in detail in Appendix 3.

Making sense of what you read

It is amazing that so many of us have gone through school, college, or even graduate school without ever being taught how to read informational material. As a result, we often have difficulty identifying the main points and really comprehending and retaining what we are reading. To ensure that we can support our students' mastery of these skills, we need to gain mastery of them ourselves. There are many things that you can do to help you read so that you will remember, understand, and be able to apply your own experiences to what you have read (see Exercise 2 at the end of the chapter).

The first thing you can do, before you start reading an article or a chapter of a book, is to look over the article/chapter to get a sense of the structure and organization of the article. This will give you an idea of where to go to find specific information in the text. To help you identify the author's main points, try underlining or highlighting what you believe are the significant sections of passages. Also, circle words that you aren't sure about. Try to find the explanation for that word or phrase in the surrounding text, and if you are still confused, look up the word in a dictionary.

Making notes in the margins of the text, on sticky notes, or on note cards about the big ideas/main points of the text can further aid your understanding of the material. If you've underlined or highlighted an important sentence, for example, rephrase this meaning for yourself in your own words in the margins or on your note cards. These notes can just consist of a phrase or maybe a word or a sentence—it depends on your preference. The important point is to be clear to yourself so you can refer to these notes later to help you understand what you read.

After you have completed all your readings, review your notes and sort them into big ideas or themes that have emerged from common issues you have identified across all the texts. Sometimes these big ideas or themes may be best categorized under your research subquestions. To identify the big ideas or themes, it helps to go back over the important points you encountered in your reading and color code them into themes. You can choose a different color highlight pen for each different theme or big idea. Then use each designated colored pen to underline or reunderline, highlight or rehighlight the words, sentences, or sections that are relevant to that color's theme. Later, when you write or discuss the literature you have read, the themes will be easier to identify and sort.

Sometimes it helps to make a chart in which you put quotes (with page numbers and other citation information) or your paraphrasing of important points (also reference the citation and page number) under the big idea the information represents. The following is an example of how such a chart might be organized:

Big idea #1	Big idea #2	Big idea #3
Quotes or information from text with full citations	Quotes or information from text with citations	Quotes or information from text with citations

You can use this same technique later when you analyze the data you collect for your own study (see Chapter 7).

Writing up your review

With your chart completed, putting your literature review together should be relatively easy because you have already organized all the information you have collected around the big themes or ideas you will be discussing. Begin your writing with an introduction that describes the big ideas or themes you have discovered in the readings. Next, devote a section for each big idea or theme, explaining and illustrating each idea with examples and quotes (if desired) from the texts you have read. Remember in these sections that you are explaining an idea and that you are *synthesizing* what you have read. (A synthesis pulls together ideas across many readings, referencing the views of the different authors to illustrate and elaborate on ideas. It is not a report that serially discusses one idea or author's work after another.)

After you have completed a section that discusses each big idea or theme, write a conclusion summarizing what you have discussed. In this section, address any differences and/or similarities you have found in the readings and discuss your own views of the issues: What have *you* learned from and what do *you* think about what these other researchers/authors have said? What is your evaluation, interpretation, or conclusion? In other words, with whom do you agree/disagree? Do you think that they have misinterpreted, ignored, underemphasized, or overemphasized particular aspects of the question? Finally, what questions are you left with after reading other peoples' work? How does this all relate to your study?

Figure 4–1 on page 51 is a guide that outlines steps to follow as you create your literature review.

Reviewing your work

After you have drafted your literature review, go over what you have written, either alone or with a colleague, to help you ensure you have done your best work. Refer to the guide in Figure 4–2 as well as to Exercise 7 at the end of the chapter for characteristics of what makes an effective and well-written literature review.

For an example of a literature review that exemplifies the qualities outlined in the figure, please refer to Appendix 4.

Searching the literature with children

The very same research skills that you use for putting together a review of the literature on your topic of interest can and should be taught to children. Although, for young children, direct inquiry with materials and experiences is generally the place to begin any investigation, it is important for them to learn how to find information from text and on-line resources as well. Everyone should have experience with this kind of research. To ensure that they do, make sure that class time is allocated during any study to browse through books and other texts. Some children will need to do this at the beginning of their studies to help clarify the focus of the research. Others may be able to wait until after their study is underway to access specific information that will extend their investigations. Children should be encouraged to use books from their class and school libraries, from the public library, as well as books they may bring from home.

In addition to books, make sure to utilize a wide range of other resources when conducting an investigation. These can include newspapers, magazines, the Internet, observations, experiments, travel, TV,

Figure 4–1. Steps to Creating Your Literature Review

1. Define the issues connected to your question that you need to read about.

2. Do a search for articles, books, websites, etc.

3. Read the information you have gathered.

   a. Highlight, underline, or make notes about the important information and ideas you have read.

   b. Create a reference list as you go, making note of all important reference information (don't forget to note the volume and issue number of periodicals as well as the pages in which the information was found).

4. Review what you marked as important and identify the big ideas or themes that cut across your reading (either in the margins, on note cards, or on sticky notes, or by color-coded highlighting).

5. Make a chart or outline of the big ideas, noting the sections in the text that fit under each big idea or theme.

6. Write up what you have learned:

   a. Write a summary introduction of the big ideas/themes.

   b. Subtitle and discuss each theme/big idea in a separate section, synthesizing and discussing the information from all your readings.

7. Write a conclusion that analyzes and draws implications about all the ideas you have discussed:

   a. How does this all connect to your study?

   b. What questions are you left with?

Figure 4–2. Literature Review Guide

Introduction

- The context/background for the literature is described.

- The big ideas or themes that you discovered in the readings are introduced in a brief overview or map so that the reader of the review can expect what to find in the rest of the review.

Big Ideas

- Each big idea or theme discovered in the readings is discussed in a separate section that has a heading.

- Each big idea is explained and illustrated with examples and quotes (if desired) from the different readings.

- Each idea discussed is relevant to your research questions.

- Different authors' writings are synthesized (not discussed in a string of separate reports) and used to illustrate different aspects of each big idea.

- Multiple and reliable data sources are referenced.

- Ideas and/or quotes from different authors are referenced.

- Correct reference format is used.

Conclusions/Implications

- The big ideas found throughout the texts are summarized.

- Differences and/or similarities in the perspective of the researchers/authors who were referenced are addressed.

- Your own views of the issues are discussed, explaining what *you* have learned from and what *you* think about what these other researchers/authors have said.

- The ideas are evaluated and interpreted. With whom do you agree/ disagree? Do you think that they have misinterpreted, ignored, underemphasized, or overemphasized particular aspects of the questions?

- How the big ideas in your review relate to the study you plan to conduct is explained.

- Questions you are left with after reading other peoples' work are articulated.

Writing

- Ideas are communicated clearly and presented in a well-organized manner.

- Mechanics and conventions of print (spelling, punctuation, grammar, etc.) are used correctly.

- Text references and end references are formatted correctly.

---

interviews, and/or trips. Most children will need assistance selecting which resources will be best suited to answer their different research questions. One way to help them is to hold a class meeting during which you all generate a list of possible resources to consult. Let the children offer the possibilities. Don't forget to remind the children that, in addition to the resources on the list, *they* can be resources to each other. They might know of books, people, or places to visit that can help each other investigate their questions. Then review different questions the children have generated and brainstorm together what resources to consult.

Trips that could be made to pursue individual studies might include visits to an art museum for a study of an artist, to a planetarium for a study of the solar system, to famous buildings for an architectural study, to a history museum for a study of ancient Egypt, to a cultural center for an investigation of one's heritage, to a zoo to pursue a study of animals, to a botanical garden to explore the rain forest. Interviews with elders can be used to study one's family history or the history of a neighborhood. Interviews with experts can be conducted to learn about a specific issue—with an architect for a study of buildings, with a scientist for a study of bubbles, with a museum curator for a study of art (Falk & Margolin, 2005).

Using the Internet with children

When gathering informational resources, don't forget to take advantage of resources on the Internet. There are several search engines designed specifically for children. Among them are

Yahooligans: *http://yahooligans.yahoo.com/*

Ask Jeeves for Kids: *www.ajkids.com*

Kids Click!: *http://sunsite3.berkeley.edu/KidsClick!/*

These sites provide understandable, age-appropriate, and user-friendly information for children. Even with these sites, however, it is still important for children to learn how to evaluate the information they are accessing on different types of sites. The suggestions and websites that give guidance to website evaluation provided in Appendix 2 can be used to help children gain awareness of these issues.

Building knowledge, developing skills

Once resource materials are identified, children need to be taught how to use the information they have collected. First they need to learn how to access information in the materials. They need to be taught how to use tables of contents, indexes, glossaries, and bibliographies so that they can know where to go in the text to find the information they need. You can hold mini lessons with your class to instruct them about each one of these elements of nonfiction texts.

Children also need guidance on how to process and understand what they are reading. Although this skill may come naturally to some, most need explicit instruction in how to highlight, underline, take notes, and/or make outlines of the important ideas in the text. An effective way to teach these techniques is to have the class all read the same passage together and highlight or underline important information. Next, have them discuss what they understood and why they highlighted or underlined some ideas rather than others. Make sure to emphasize how to distinguish point of view from fact and how to interpret the information. You can do this same kind of activity with different passages for teaching note-taking and/or outlining skills. After completing these exercises, everyone should be better equipped to understand and retain what has been read (Falk & Margolin, 2005).

Similar activities can be done to teach how to organize/synthesize the big ideas of readings, how to analyze the information, and how to write introductions and conclusions. Each step of the way needs to be scaffolded for children with explicit directions and criteria that make the image of accomplished work crystal clear.

Working in this way with the children in your class, you can help them learn the necessary skills in the context of studies in a way that honors their views and ideas. You will be amazed at how their reading and writing skills develop when they get to use them in meaningful ways.

Exercise 1: Developing key words or concepts for conducting a search

Fill in the following chart:

Concept 1	and	Concept 2	and	Concept 3
or		or		or
or		or		or
not		not		not

Exercise 2: Questions for evaluating a website

1. Who is the author of the site? If the author is one person, what are that person's credentials? If the author is an organization, check it out in the *Encyclopedia of Associations* in your library. Is there an address or e-mail address given?

2. What country or state does this website come from?

3. How objective is the website? What is its purpose—to inform you, convince you of a point of view, sell you a product or service, amuse or entertain you?

4. How current is the website's content? Has it been updated to reflect current news and trends? Check the date of creation, the last update, and if the links are up-to-date.

5. Who is the intended audience for the site? At what age or reading level is it aimed?

6. How is the site organized? Is it organized logically? Is it well designed? Is it easy to navigate? Does it overwhelm you with ads?

Exercise 3: Making sense of what you read

Here are some tips for how to read and take notes actively so that you remember, understand, and are able to apply to your own experiences what you have read:

- Look over the article/chapter to get a sense of the structure and organization of the article.

- As you read the text, underline, highlight, or put sticky notes on significant passages that you think represent the main points of what you have read.

- Circle words that you aren't sure about and find the explanation for that word.

- Jot down the main points of the author in the margins or on note cards (using your own words) as you read.

Exercise 4: Analyzing what you read

Ask yourself the following questions about each article that you read:

- Who is saying this?

- From what perspective?

- Does it make sense?

- Do I agree or disagree?

- Did I "buy" it?

- Why or why not?

- What exactly do I agree with? What exactly do I disagree with?

- What other thoughts do I have about what I have read?

Exercise 5a: Sorting the big ideas across articles

• Color code the big ideas or themes you encountered in your reading. Choose a different color highlight pen for each different theme or big idea, then underline words, sentences, or sections that are relevant to each theme.

• After you have finished reading, sort the big ideas you have identified in the chart provided here:

Big idea #1	Big idea #2	Big idea #3

Exercise 5b: Sorting the big ideas across articles— Another way

• Read and reread your notes, or sticky notes, or highlighted sections in your articles and chapters.

• Write each of the emerging big ideas on the top of a separate index card.

• Go back through the articles and note what different authors say about the big idea on the appropriate index card.

• Take the cards and move them around in different orders. What seems to make sense?

• When you are comfortable with the order, write it down in an outline and then fill in more notes, if needed, to make your outline more complete.

Exercise 6: Questions for helping you synthesize ideas

• What are the ideas or perspectives that the authors you have read have in common? Explain with examples.

• How do the ideas or perspectives of the different authors differ? Explain with examples.

Exercise 7: Guide for reviewing a literature review

Introduction

- Did you describe the context/background for the literature that is being reviewed?

- Did you begin the review of the literature with an introduction of the big ideas or themes that you discovered in the readings?

- In other words, did you create a brief overview or map for the reader of what he/she should expect to find in the review?

Big Ideas

- Did you provide a separate section with a heading for each big idea or theme?

- In each section, did you explain the big idea and illustrate it with examples and quotes (if desired) from the different readings?

- Are each of the subsections relevant to your research questions?

- Did you synthesize different authors' writings to illustrate different aspects of each big idea (not discuss their work as separate reports)?

- Did you reference the ideas or quotes from different authors?

- Did you use multiple and reliable sources?

- Did you use the correct reference format?

Conclusions/Implications

- Did you summarize the big ideas found throughout the texts, addressing any differences and/or similarities in the perspective of the researchers/authors read?

- Did you discuss your own views of the issues, explaining what *you* have learned from and what *you* think about what these other researchers/authors have said?

- Did you present your evaluation, interpretation, or conclusion? With whom do you agree/disagree: Do you think that they have misinterpreted, ignored, underemphasized, or overemphasized particular aspects of the questions?

- Did you explain how the big ideas in your review relate to your study?

- Did you articulate any questions you are left with after reading other peoples' work?

Writing

- Are your ideas communicated clearly and presented in a well-organized manner?

- Have you used the mechanics and conventions of print (spelling, punctuation, grammar, etc.) correctly?

- Have you used the in-text reference and end reference format correctly?

Exercise 8: Steps to follow to help children make sense of what they have read

- Have the class all read the same passage.

- Ask each student to highlight or underline important information.

- Lead a discussion about what they understood and why they highlighted or underlined some ideas rather than others.

- Emphasize how to distinguish point of view from fact and how to interpret information.

- Repeat the activity with a different passage, adding note-taking and/or outlining skills, or how to organize/synthesize the big ideas of what has been read.

Five

The Research Design
Developing an Action Plan
for Your Inquiry

● ● ●

Research is formalized curiosity.
It is poking and prying with purpose.

—Zora Neale Hurston

*A*fter exploring what others know about your question, making a plan of action for your own study can help you proceed with your investigation. Although it may be tempting just to jump right in and begin collecting data, developing a plan will give you a working document to help you ensure that your research is sound—that it is systematic, based on evidence, and credible. Once this plan is developed, however, it should not remain static. Rather, it should serve as a flexible guide throughout the life of your study. Just as the ideas and interactions of your students influence and alter your curriculum plans in the classroom, the data you collect during the course of your inquiry should inform and shape how you proceed.

Your research design should flow from your question and subquestions. Everything you decide to do should be aimed at getting answers to these questions. But before you begin your exploration, you need to consider and make decisions about *how* you will proceed. The following is an outline of what you need to figure out:

Research design

    1. Statement and explanation of your research question

        a. The research question and subquestions

b. Overview of what you plan to do in your study

c. Context and background for your study

2. Methodology

a. A description of the study participants and setting

b. Data sources

c. Data collection plans

d. Data analysis plans

3. Time line for your study

4. References

Making this plan will help you clarify exactly who and what you will study as well as when and how you will study it. It will also help you start to think about how you will analyze the evidence you collect. The decisions you make about each one of these issues will impact what you will learn from your investigation.

Relevant data

When you formulated your research question and subquestions, you also developed an overview of how you plan to approach your study and prepared an explanation of the background and context that influenced your choice. Now you need to work out the details of how you are going to find answers to your questions.

Who are you going to study? ○ The first thing to determine is exactly who you are going to study. In research terms this is called *defining your study participants* or *sample*. The nature of your question and what you decide to do to pursue answers to your question will greatly impact who you examine. For example, when teacher researcher Cristina Castellon studied the impact of inclusion on both regular and special education students, it was fitting for her to explore her question by looking at all the students in her class:

> I looked at the regular education and the special education students in my first grade classroom in the South Bronx. I looked at twenty-one children ranging in age from six to seven years. The demographics of the class consist of Latino and black students with one Guyanese child.

For Michael's study of discipline, it also was appropriate to focus on the dynamics among all the children in his class:

> I studied my class and to a lesser degree the other 5/6s class in our school. We share deck time with the other class so it gave me an opportunity to test management strategies on students other than my own.

However, when teacher researcher Loretta Francis was investigating discipline techniques for difficult children, she focused her study on only those children in her class who were a challenge in that regard.

Sometimes decisions about whom to study are made for reasons of feasibility. If your question lends itself to focus on a select group, it is important that you describe who you have selected to study and what criteria you used for your selection. Teacher researcher Matthew Steinberg did this in his study of how to foster student engagement in his fifth grade classroom. He explained:

> I selected six students ... from among the thirty students in my class because of their observed level of motivation. I identified two students who were at the low end of the spectrum, two students who fell in the middle range, and two students at the high end of motivation. These students were chosen as a result of my observations of their level of engagement during the first six months of school. [I looked at] their participation in class discussions, the thoroughness and effort on their assignments, both in class and out, as well as the students' initiative in beginning and working on class assignments.

Bridgette, too, decided to study only four of the girls in her class for her inquiry about the impact of single-sex literature circles on female students. As she described the girls she chose and how she selected them, she provided details about each one:

> The participants of this research study are four girls in my seventh grade literacy class. Although all the girls score well on statewide standardized assessments and receive high marks in literacy class, they have differing social and reading habits.

Julie is a very avid reader but only when reading very specific novels of her own choosing. She is vocal in large-group
discussions, although not nearly as vocal as the four or five
dominant boys in the class, and is popular with the boys and
girls in her class.

Alex is also an avid reader who enjoys many types of books,
although mostly contemporary novels with a female heroine.
She is silent in class discussions, almost never participating, especially in open-ended, thinking discussions. Her family pushes
Alex to read, even creating a book club for her and her friends.

Ginny has the highest grade and test scores in her class, and
participates less than Julie and more than Alex. She is a reluctant reader, citing mystery as her favorite genre, although usually during independent reading time she appears to be day-
dreaming rather than entranced in her book.

Lastly, Kristin is a leader of her peers in social situations, and
appears to be more reserved and contemplative than many of
the other students. She is often silent in large-group situations,
but always appears attentive with her chair posture, consistent
note taking, and eye contact. She reads well but her reading is
usually during assigned periods, rather than self-initiated.

I chose this sample of girls to be in the single-sex literature circle partially due to their exhibited success in literacy class. I
felt their high reading ability would lend itself to less disciplining to make the girls complete their assigned readings and to
more available time for discussion and debate. In addition,
the girls' differing reading and social habits promise to provide a full picture of how an all-girl literature circle can affect
the girls' enjoyment and comfort in discussion of a book.

Notice how Bridgette included, in her description of her study participants, only as much background information as was needed to provide a
context of her study. This is also what Michelle did to describe the child she
studied for her investigation of how to support a child with special needs:

The participant in this study is Kareem—a five-year-old,
African American boy who has a speech impediment, and

who was [diagnosed] at two years old as developmentally delayed in language acquisition through an evaluation by state evaluators. He did receive related services when he was four years old but no longer receives related services because he has "aged out" of the program. It is now the responsibility of his parents to get outside services. His mother is a part-time cashier, mother of three, and attends a junior college. His father lives in the household and does not work.

Notice here how Michelle did not reveal the identity of her study participants and how she provided background information in a factual manner, avoiding judgments, evaluative statements, and/or details about the child and his family. This is important to watch out for. What you choose to include or not include about your research participants, as well as how you convey that information, are all conscious or unconscious interpretations and acts of analysis that impact the study's credibility (Geertz, 1973).

This is especially important for all of us to keep in mind when working with people who come from backgrounds that are different than our own or who have different perspectives other than our own. Our own backgrounds and philosophies of education can influence how data are presented and viewed. That is why it is helpful to provide information about yourself and your own background as you describe your study's participants, especially if you are a "participant–observer" (i.e., your study is about your work in your class). Doing so will make it easier for others to understand and interpret your findings. Michelle explained herself as the participant–observer this way:

I was also a participant in this study as a researcher and observer. I am a twenty-nine-year-old African American teacher who has worked in the early childhood field for ten years, but has never worked with young children who have special needs up until now.

Describe the setting of your study ◦ A description of the context of your study helps to inform others about how to interpret your findings. This section of your research design may include a description of the school setting, the outside community, and the classrooms or other settings where the study is taking place. A description of your study's setting can also help you think through the potential benefits and pitfalls of the setting and clarify what aspects of the setting might affect your data collection process.

Jumel's description of his school setting was critical to understanding his study of his sixth grade students' feelings about using Standard English in school. He obtained statistics to provide a portrait of his school and community:

> Intermediate school XXX is located in the Upper Manhattan area of Harlem. I.S. XXX shares the school building with elementary school XXX. The school consists of approximately 470 students. It is on the state's S.U.R.R. (School Under Registration Review) list, which means that I.S. XXX is a low-performing public school that is targeted for corrective action. The school supposedly runs the risk of being closed if significant improvements are not made. Eighty-three percent of the students are "African Americans." Fifteen percent of the students are "Latino" children and 2% are "Other." The students live in public housing projects and other neighboring buildings located around the school.

Note that Jumel avoided using the school's name and purposely did not provide information that would help readers identify it. Later, in his story about his class, he also protected the privacy of his study's participants by using pseudonyms instead of real names.

What data will you collect? ○ Among the data sources most commonly used by teachers for their classroom inquiries are observations, interviews, pictures, videotapes, audiotapes, journals, surveys, samples of student work, and other documents. (These data collection tools will be discussed more thoroughly in Chapter 6.) As you think about which of these you will collect for your study, there are two important things to remember. The first is to use your research questions to guide your choice of which kind of data to collect. Think about how each data source you decide to use will answer each one of your questions. One way to help you figure this out is to make a chart that lists your research question and subquestions in the left column, with your data collection tools across the top. Make Xs in the chart to explain what data source will give you answers to what questions (see Figure 5–1 and Exercise 1 at the end of the chapter).

It is also important to remember, as you decide what evidence you will collect for your study, that you will need to use multiple data sources to pursue your question. A minimum of three different sources is generally recommended. This "triangulation" of data helps you see things from multiple perspectives and thus adds to the reliability and validity of your findings.

Triangulating your data can be done in different ways: studying a phenomenon through *multiple data techniques* (for instance, collecting observations, audiotapes, and photographs) or looking at a situation from the *multiple points of view* of the participants involved (such as caregivers, students, and teachers).

Here is an example of how Shenaz decided to triangulate data for her study of how to make her reading and writing conferences more effective. First she described how each data source would help to answer her questions. Then she made the chart (Figure 5–1). She chose different *kinds* of data sources that would provide her with different kinds of information about her students and her teaching:

I am going to collect the following data: personal journal, student work, conference notes, and formal assessments.

The *conference notes* that I will collect will reveal to me what I have learned about each student and what I have taught them. As time progresses, the notes should reveal more about me and how I conferred with each student. These notes will also show me the direction my mini lessons are going to go. Over time I should be able to see in my conference notes if children are using the strategies and skills I have taught them, and as a result how they grow as readers and writers.

I will also reflect in a *personal journal*. This journal will allow me to take a deeper look into how each of my conferences went. It will show the growth in my conferring. The journal will allow me to learn what my strengths are in conferring with my students. It will also point out the areas that I need to improve and begin to work on them, such as shortening my conferences or making better teaching decisions.

My *students' work* will also show the growth in my conferencing. I should be able to see explicitly in their writing over time how they have grown through my one-to-one teaching. Their work will also reveal to me what I need to teach them during our conferences. As I evaluate their reading I will see the children using the strategies I have taught them in our reading conferences. The same will go for their writing, which will reveal in what area each child needs help, therefore allowing me to focus on that area during our conferences.

The children's growth should also show in the *formal assessments* I will use. The beginning of the year formal in-class assessment will be compared with the one given in the spring.

Figure 5–1. How Data Aligns with Subquestions Chart

Subquestions	Data 1 personal journal	Data 2 student work	Data 3 conference notes	Data 4 formal assessment
How do I manage conferences in a Reading and Writing Workshop?	X		X	
What do you do in a reading and writing conference?	X	X	X	
What do you do with the information you gain from conferring with students in a Reading and Writing Workshop?	X	X		
How does conferring with students help them become better readers and writers?	X	X	X	X

A different rationale for the choice of data sources was given by teacher researcher Swati Mehta for her examination of how the concept of identity developed in three adolescent Indian American women. Because she was trying to understand the young women's perspectives on their identity, she decided to collect data that would give her different windows into their thinking: observations, interviews, and the participants' writing samples. Swati's explanation of her data collection and analysis process demonstrates how her choices matched the purpose of her research questions and the theoretical framework of her study:

This study is qualitative in its nature. The data were collected through three means: observation, interview, and the writing of the participants. The data were collected to inform me in different ways about how these women perceived their lives. Observation allowed the reality to be expressed through their experience. Interviews allowed the voices of the participants and their parents to surface. Writing, finally, allowed a personal expression of the participants' thoughts and feelings about identity. The purpose was thus to weave together the lives of these women through the lens of seeing them as multicultural, with multiidentities, and multirealities. The purpose was not to place judgment, and thus data were not looked at for finding cultural contradictions within the lives of these women. Instead, I aimed to understand the truths that these women created. As a result of the framework, typed-up notes and final narrative stories and analysis were shared with all three participants to establish a way to cross-check the data that led to their unique identity stories.

Swati's decision to have the participants "cross-check" her data analysis was one more way to ensure that she was getting these women's perspectives on their identities.

How will you collect your data? ● In addition to figuring out what data you will collect for your study, you also need to make plans for who will collect the data, where and when each type of data will be collected, and how long the data collection process will go on (see Exercise 2 at the end of the chapter).

Try to think through the specifics about the time of day (and dates if possible) that you will collect data, the area of the room or the curriculum time where you will collect the data, and exactly how you will be collecting it (if notes, in a notebook?). If, for instance, you are making observations, plan how often you would like to observe and how you will focus the observations. If you plan to conduct a survey or if you are interviewing, think through the questions you will ask, who you will survey or interview, where the interviews will take place, and how long you might expect each session to last. (More details about how to figure out these issues can be found in Chapter 6.)

Here is how Shenaz planned to collect data for her study of reading and writing conferences:

> I will collect all my data for approximately eight to ten weeks. The conferences and formal assessments will take place during the Reading and Writing Workshop periods within my classroom. During this same time I will collect my conference notes. My personal journal, however, will not be done during Reading and Writing Workshop. I will write in my journal each day after school when I have time to sit and look through any conference notes and reflect without distractions.

Bridgette described her data collection methods for her study of all-girl literature circles in this way:

> I will collect my data in about four weeks in the K–8 school in which I work. I will collect the data in two ways: First, I will observe the girls during our regular class periods three times for approximately thirty minutes each, while they and the other thirty students are engaged in literature circles. Then I will meet with the girls in our classroom during lunch or another noninstructional period three times to discuss my observations. I will also collect written responses from each girl on a rolling basis throughout this period.

Ethical concerns

As you plan the kind of data you will collect, it is important that you take care to be respectful of your study's participants. Although you may be clear that the purpose of your inquiry is to understand and improve your practice, this goal may not be apparent to those you are studying. So before you begin, it is best to inform those who are involved about your intentions and to get their permission to allow you to study them. They always have a right to refuse to be the focus of your attention. You can do this with a permission letter, often referred to as *informed consent.*

Now, it may *not* be necessary to get permission for the data you collect if you plan to use what you learn from your study only for your own or your students' growth and development. For instance, collecting student work for diagnostic purposes and keeping notes on classroom activities for the purpose of shaping your curriculum and meeting students' needs do not require permission because these activities are simply a part of good teaching. However, if you intend to share the information you are collecting with a wider audience—to present at a districtwide conference, a professional symposium, or to write for publication—there are several important reasons why permission should be obtained from those who are the subject of study.

One reason is that study participants need to be informed if your study has the potential to expose them to any harm or risk. This concern is greatest in experimental studies, during which a potentially harmful or helpful intervention or treatment may be applied to or withheld from one group and not another. Although harm to study participants is unlikely in the kind of naturalistic, qualitative study you are doing, because only natural events are being documented, the mere fact that something is being studied *can* affect what happens. So, in addition to doing your best not to let your study impact anyone's experiences negatively, you need to assure all those involved about any possible potential for harm to occur.

A second reason to ask permission to carry out your study has to do with concerns about privacy. Even if anonymity is ensured by using pseudonyms instead of participants' real names (which should always be standard procedure if you intend to share your work publicly), potential study participants may not want you to take work samples, photos, or videos of them or their child for personal, religious, or other reasons. So check to make sure that it is OK to do this.

Yet another reason to obtain consent is that some people may be wary of how they will be perceived or represented by you, the researcher. This is understandable given the bias, discussed earlier, that we sometimes unwittingly bring to what we see and do.

And finally, participants need to be assured that their involvement in the study is purely voluntary—that should they decide not to be involved, they will be not be treated negatively by you in any way.

Once you have considered all these issues, craft a permission letter to those involved in your study. Before doing this, check to see if your school or school district has policies on research in the classroom. There may be an official approval process that you must go through. Or, you may find that your administrator wants to be involved in the construction of your consent forms. In any case, be sure that your consent letter explains your study and its purpose; includes information about the data collection process, possible risks, and the potential benefits the study might yield; efforts you will make to protect the participants' privacy; and assurances that involvement is voluntary and participants, at any time without any negative consequences, may decide that they do not want to be involved.

You can find out more information about how to craft and administer research consent forms on most university websites, because university researchers have to get approval for any study they undertake from their institution's institutional review board. You can also find a permission request template available for your use in one of the websites listed in Appendix 5 or at *www.landmark-project.com/permission1.php.*

On the next page is an example of a consent form that teacher researcher Nkenge Mayfield sent home to the families in her class before embarking on a study of how to use unit blocks in her early childhood classroom. Notice how the letter is written in easily understandable language.

There are a few more things to think about and plan for before you begin to collect data for your study. You need to consider how you will go about analyzing your data and what time frame you will follow to complete your study.

How will you go about analyzing your data?
Considering how you will analyze your data is an important part of your research plan. Before developing this section of your plan, you might want to read Chapter 7, which discusses data analysis in greater detail and provides you with specific procedures for how to draw conclusions from your evidence. But now you need to think about how to use the data you collect in your study not only to draw conclusions at your study's end, but also to inform and shape it as it unfolds. Reviewing your data in an ongoing way throughout the process of your study can help you to formulate impressions and hunches, grow theories, and evolve themes that will affect how you proceed. This ongoing analysis may lead you to look at things you might not have planned to examine, to talk to people you might not have thought of interviewing, or to collect evidence you might have not thought was necessary.

Dear Families,

I am working on a study this year of how I can use unit blocks in our class curriculum to enhance children's development. Although the project is in the early stages of development, I anticipate that I'll be looking at the children's play with blocks, taking pictures of their structures, and, from time to time, recording their conversations while in the block area. I also will be making copies of some of the children's writings and drawings, with their permission. The purpose of this documentation will be to give me a chance to examine closely the children at work in the block area in a way I cannot ordinarily do in the midst of the busy classroom day. I hope that this study will help me better understand how to use blocks more effectively to support the children's learning in our classroom.

Although I don't know, as of yet, what exactly I will or will not include in my study, I would like to have your permission to use the information I learn from your child, as well as any photographs of your child or any writing or drawing that your child might make. I do not foresee any risks to your child from participating in this study. And please be assured that in any reports using this research, a fictitious name will be used to protect your child's privacy.

Please sign this form and return it to me by_____. Should you decide that you do not want your child to participate, your decision will not be held against you in any way. Should you agree to participate but change your mind later, your wishes will be respected.

Thank you very much.

Your child's teacher

_____

I give permission for my child to participate in the study on blocks.

_____   _____
Child's name   Parent's signature
(please print first and last name)

Date: _____

Although it is not possible to figure out completely all the details of your data analysis until you have settled on your questions and collected your data, you want to make sure your analysis plan includes ideas for how to organize and review the data as you proceed. As you learn more about your research topic and your study develops, this plan will change and get more detailed. Begin here, however, by thinking about how you will use the data you collect to inform your study in an ongoing way, how you will organize your data as you collect it, at what points in the data collection process you will review/analyze it, and what method you will use to analyze your data and develop your findings (see Exercise 3 at the end of the chapter).

Here is how Shenaz first thought about how she would analyze the data she collected for her study of reading and writing conferences. Because she wrote this at the beginning of her study, she had a clear idea of how she would review and use her data to inform her teaching and the progression of her study, but she had not yet developed the details about how she would come up with the overall findings of her study.

I plan to look over my conference notes every week so I can determine what mini lessons I need to plan for the following week. In my conference notes I comment on what the students are doing, and if they are doing what I taught them in their last conference. This allows me to determine if my students are learning and implementing what I have taught them.

In my personal journal I reflect at least three times a week on my conferences for the day. I record in my journal what I think I did well and what I need to work on. Reviewing it every two weeks will allow me to determine what I need to work on and what I am getting better at.

My students' work will be reviewed every two weeks. I analyze student work before I have taught something in a conference and then compare it with student work a couple weeks later. This allows me to determine whether they are applying the strategies I have taught them during my conferences.

Finally, I will collect and review the district's formal in-class assessment in March at the end of my study to see if the students have grown in their reading and writing.

The following analysis plan, developed by Natalie for her study of how to support her students' independent learning in centers, focuses on both formative and summative data analysis. In her description of her plan she explains how she will use a chart (below) both to analyze and store the data she will collect for each of her research subquestions. (See Chapter 7 for a more detailed explanation of how to create a data analysis chart.)

The themes I will use for organizing (coding) my data are the topics of my subquestions:

1. Evidence of children being their own teachers
2. Evidence of play in centers impacting development
3. Anecdotals used to drive teaching
4. Extensions of mini lessons in play

I will assign a different color to each theme and use a chart like the following to keep my dated observations, photos, and work samples organized.

Evidence Collection Chart

Evidence of:			
Children as their own teachers	Play in centers impacting development	Anecdotals used to drive teaching	Extensions of mini lessons in play

By using this chart as an ongoing tool for analysis, I will be able to note which areas might be lacking data and I can then focus my observations on these areas. As I fill in the chart, I will be beginning the process of analyzing my data. I will look for patterns in my observations and evidence of the social, physical, emotional, and behavioral development of children in centers. I will also use this chart to do an overall, final analysis when all my data are collected.

Teacher researcher Melissa Sugrim's data analysis plan for her study of developmentally appropriate literacy practices explains how she will organize her evidence around her research subquestions and how she will label and color code the evidence for each subquestion. (This process is explained in detail in Chapter 7.)

> I will read through all my data, which will include my observations, photos, samples of children's work, and my reflections on all these. I will then organize my data according to their various themes or categories, and then color code my data to highlight those observations and reflections that are associated with each specific theme or category. For example, a highlight of green will indicate environmental support of literacy, a highlight of blue will indicate teaching practices/strategies that support developmentally appropriate practices in literacy, and a highlight of pink will indicate how the curriculum supports developmentally appropriate practices in literacy. Next, I will revisit my data to ensure that all data have been color coded accordingly. Each reflection will be numbered and every work sample and photo labeled. Work samples will be labeled S1, S2, S3, etc. Photos will be labeled P1, P2, P3, and so forth. The next steps will be to match these work samples and photos with their supporting reflections.

In contrast, teacher researcher Sheri Rothman's plan for her study about how to increase students' problem-solving abilities in mathematics, explains how she will organize her data not around subquestions, but around themes that emerge through the course of the study. Note how she also describes her process for ongoing analysis and organization of her data.

> Because I will be keeping all my interview and field notes in a spiral notebook, it will be easier for me to analyze them. The notebook has a built-in margin on each page where I can notate general categories for each piece of information. Categorizing notes in the margins will help me to get an idea of what is in the notes, in what order, and will provide me with a way to reference something quickly just by scanning the side of the page.

I will also create an index to help me narrow my focus. I will list all categories and the pages in my notes where they appear. It will help me to see how often certain categories appear. I will also free write on the categories that appear the most often, so that I can see what patterns and themes emerge.

I will probably use my journal to write narrative memos that help me to capture thoughts and ideas that I don't want to forget. The memos hopefully will allow me to see what direction to move next.

Although these data analysis plans describe different ways to analyze data, they are similar in that they each help the teacher inquirers who wrote them to think through in advance what they plan to do.

Creating a time line for your study

Creating a time line is a useful strategy to help you make sure you complete your study. We all know how easy it is to procrastinate and how life inadvertently gets in the way of even some of the best-laid plans. Thinking in advance about the time it will take to get things done can help you stick to your intentions. Because your inquiry may be affected by so many things outside your own will or control (school holidays, vacations, school testing days, unforeseen school or personal events), planning around them in advance, to the extent that you can, will help you get a realistic sense of the challenges you will face and how you can proceed.

An important issue to consider when planning the time frame for your study is whether the question that interests you now will be important or even feasible to investigate when you are ready and able to collect data. This issue came up for one teacher researcher who got interested in separation anxiety at the beginning of the school year when one of the children in her early childhood class was having trouble beginning the school day and separating from his mother. She reconsidered her choice of questions, however, as she realized that the period of the child's separation difficulties could (hopefully for everyone involved) be short and not leave her enough time to do the kind of in-depth investigation that she wanted to do.

To help you figure out things like these, sketch a plan for when and how much time you will need to collect your data, analyze the data, review the literature about your question, draft your findings and conclusions, and revise what you have done for the final draft. Make sure that you build in time to review your evidence frequently so that you can see repeating patterns, share your thoughts with others, feel confident about your emerging findings, and put care into how you draft and revise what you have learned (see Exercise 4 at the end of the chapter).

Your time line should look something like this one that Natalie created to pace herself through her study:

December: Construct my research design and begin my literature review.

January: Work on my literature review and begin collecting data.

February/March: Continue collecting data, reviewing/coding/ analyzing once a week.

Mid-March: Analyze all the data for findings and conclusions.

April/May: Write first draft of what I have found, revise, and write a final draft.

As you make your plans, remember that things always take longer than you think. So keep your schedule flexible. Along the way, expect that you will get frustrated or confused, or that your questions may evolve and change. Don't be surprised if you realize at some point that the data you are collecting are not providing evidence that will answer your questions. And don't despair if your emerging ideas and understandings are difficult to express in written form. Expect setbacks to happen and changes to be needed. It is all part of the messy process of learning in uncharted terrain.

Citing your references

As you make the plan for your study, you will likely want to consult other literature related to your question. You read about how to do this and how to create a reference list in Chapter 4. Although you may not complete a full review of the literature prior to formulating your research design, you will at least want to gather a list of the references you will consult. Other people's studies of your question may give you ideas for how to investigate it. Writings about your topic may offer suggestions that you may want to try out and examine in your investigation. From the beginning, don't forget to keep track of all the details about the sources (volume number, issue number, pages, etc.) that you will need for your reference list.

Reviewing your work: Consulting with a critical friend

As you may have experienced in your work with students, peer consultation and editing offer a powerful opportunity to share and fine-tune your ideas in a safe and constructive environment. During all our inquiries, as either teachers or researchers, having a "critical friend" with whom to share ideas, teaching strategies, curriculum plans, or research drafts can be an invaluable support to our learning.

Working with others who are either tackling similar issues in their classrooms or conducting their own studies can be very helpful. Finding a "critical friend" who can review and talk with you about your design in draft form can help you to uncover new ideas or find potential blind spots. A critical friend can suggest ways to "tighten" the design or help you make sure that each element of your plan makes sense. Exercise 5 at the end of the chapter offers some questions your critical friend can ask as he or she reviews your research design.

As your study progresses, other questions may emerge that you can bring to your critical friend. Don't be afraid to use others as a sounding board for your questions and to let ideas that develop throughout the process transform the elements of your initial design. Inquiry is not a linear process.

Planning inquiry projects for children

Children's questions are windows into their thinking and an ideal entry point for planning curriculum. To do this effectively we first need to inquire ourselves about what they understand, the problems they encounter, the strengths they bring to their learning, and then use these understandings to shape the curriculum as well as inform our instructional strategies. Only when we build into our teaching plans a way to take into account what is happening with our students—through a continual gathering of evidence of what they understand and how they can actually apply their understandings—will we have a way to assess the effectiveness of our teaching, make adjustments to what we do, and heighten the likelihood that learning will occur.

It is not easy to teach in this way given current pressures from high-stakes accountability systems and the resulting emphasis on standardization in schools. The mandated curricula and pacing schedules many of us are forced to deal with offer little opportunity for us to attend to the different paces and learning styles, understandings, interests, or questions of the students we teach. Because of this, we are often unable to take advantage of teachable moments or be responsive to what our students know and can do. And yet, children cannot learn if teachers are not able to respond to their emerging interests, struggles, misunderstandings, or wonderings. If we are to help learners genuinely learn, their thinking must be able to impact the curriculum. To do this, a balance needs to be struck between the goals and expectations of the larger community and the questions and interests children have (Falk, 2000).

Planning for a group study

Below we describe a process for how to create a plan for a group study that is built on children's questions and simultaneously prepares children to meet the standards and expectations of the external world (Falk, 2000).

After you have invited your students to brainstorm their questions and related subquestions (see Chapter 3), you will need to think through several issues. Review the questions raised by the children and search among them for commonalities. These can be crafted into a theme that can serve as the launching point for a whole-class investigation. For example, your class' previous brainstorming sessions may have raised questions about how airplanes fly, what makes electricity go on, or how water gets to our homes through the faucet. These kinds of questions could be pulled together under the rubric of an investigation into "how things work." Or your class may have asked about how seeds grow, how babies develop, how caterpillars turn into butterflies. These questions could be crafted into a study of "transformations." Coming up with an overarching theme that truly incorporates your students' authentic questions is an art that can be both challenging and fun.

Whatever the theme of the study you create, you can have the class pursue it through group activities as well as individual investigations. As you ponder the different ways to explore, think about the concepts, skills, and disciplinary knowledge that you want (and need) to infuse into the study (see Exercise 6 at the end of the chapter). This will help you generate ideas for how to structure opportunities throughout the study for the children to practice and to acquire desired goals. Think also about the "dispositions" you want to help your students develop. If you want them to become critical thinkers, life-long learners, and responsible citizens, then you will need to build experiences into the study that will nurture these kinds of qualities.

After you have attained some clarity about the goals and purposes for your plan, sketch out experiences, activities, projects, and experiments that will help your students examine the concepts, learn the skills, and develop the dispositions that you intend the study to nurture (see Exercise 7 at the end of the chapter). As you go about this process, try to plan and sequence the learning experiences to capitalize on what you know about your students' interests and their developing skills. Plan also for activities that utilize many different learning modalities so that children in your class with a range of talents and strengths will be afforded opportunities to use them. Think about how you can incorporate out-of-school activities, such as trips or interviews, to enrich the learning of the study. You might want to arrange for the class to do some kind of community service or you might want to set up a relationship with another class in the school or an outside institution. Think also about how you can involve your students' families in the inquiry. Brainstorm ideas for homework assignments that can deepen and extend class learning as well as strengthen the home/school partnership and bring families into the learning adventure.

Consider also the resources—books, materials, technology, etc.—you will need to support the work. Gathering materials or information about how to access the particular resources your study will require will increase the likelihood that your learning environment is provisioned for optimal learning.

When you have considered all these issues, review what you have designed in relation to the standards and content areas that you are required to address (see Exercise 8 at the end of the chapter). Making a grid, like the one in Figure 5–2, can be a helpful way to keep track of this information.

After the grid is made and you review it, you might find that there is a discipline area or required standard that you have not included in your study design. By planning in advance in this way, you have time to find a way to address what is missing.

As you finalize your plans, make sure that you have built in ways to assess students' progress (see Exercise 9 at the end of the chapter). Checking in with students to find out their developing ideas, to learn the

Figure 5–2. Matching Activities to Standards and Content Areas

Activity	Language arts	Math	Social studies	Science	The arts	Physical education
Activity 1	X		X		X	
Activity 2		X		X		
Activity 3	X	X	X			
Activity 4		X				X

questions that arise or the problems that come up during the course of their work, or to elicit their suggestions for what to do next can provide you with information to shape instruction more effectively. Figure 5–3 offers an example of a response sheet you can develop to ascertain this information.

By regularly reviewing students' ongoing assignments, collecting response sheets that update you on students' progress, and inviting them to air their ideas and questions at class meetings, you can nip problems in the bud and lessen the possibility that students will not "fall through the cracks."

Plan also for some kind of a culminating experience for your study (ideas for this will be discussed in Chapter 8). This will provide evidence of what children have learned through their investigations as well as build community and a sense of accomplishment.

Helping students create plans for their individual inquiries

As we discussed in the previous chapters, individual inquiries offer opportunities to experience the power of doing work that is intrinsically motivating. Providing time in your classroom for your students to engage in individual investigations can serve not only as motivators to learning, but as a way to balance individual needs with the needs and demands of the whole group. Individual studies can be conducted as extensions of a whole-group study or as stand-alone, individualized projects that enable students to engage in learning that is tailored to their interests and skill levels.

One way to help children design their own inquiry projects is to have them create project folders that include personal agendas and planning logs (see Exercises 10 and 11 at the end of the chapter). The aim of a personal agenda is to break down a project into small manageable pieces (Tomlinson, 1999). In the personal agenda each student can outline the tasks that are needed to carry out his/her investigation. Some of these tasks may require working in groups, such as peer editing; other tasks may be strictly independent work. Each student can keep the agenda in his/her individual project folder. A planning log can also accompany the agenda. On the planning log each student can chart his/her daily progress on the tasks outlined in the planning agenda. Personal agendas and planning logs allow students to take charge of their own learning. In addition, they enable tasks to be differentiated for difficulty, and instruction to be individualized to meet the needs and strengths of all the different learners in a class (Tomlinson, 1999).

Figure 5–3. Student Response Form

From this session/class I take away:

I really liked:

I am confused about:

Questions I have that still need to be answered:

Ideas about what to do next:

© 2005 by Beverly Falk and Megan Blumenreich from *The Power of Questions* (Portsmouth, NH: Heinemann).

Exercise 1: Connecting data collection techniques with research questions

In Figure 5–1 we provided an example of how a teacher researcher used a chart to connect her proposed data collection methods to her sub-questions. As you consider different sources, place them on a chart like the one that follows. Write your subquestions down the left side of the chart and think through the data sources in terms of these questions. Mark the sources that have the potential to answer aspects of the questions. In addition, write an explanation of exactly how each data source will inform the subquestions. If a data source will not help you answer your questions, don't use it.

Subquestions	Data 1	Data 2	Data 3	Data 4

Exercise 2: Planning how to collect your data

Answer the following questions as you work out your data collection plan:

- Who will collect the data?
- Where will you collect each type of data?
- When will you collect each type of data?
- For how long will you collect the data?

Exercise 3: Planning how to analyze your data

Answer the following questions as you work out your data analysis plan:

- How will you use the data you collect to inform your study in an ongoing way?
- How will you organize your data as you collect it?
- At what points in the data collection process will you review/analyze it?
- What method will you use to analyze your data and develop your findings?

Exercise 4: Creating a time line for your study

When will you do the following:

- Collect your data
- Conduct a formative analysis of your data
- Conduct a summative analysis of your data
- Review the literature about your question
- Draft your findings and conclusions
- Share your work with others for feedback
- Revise what you have done for the final draft

Exercise 5: Guide for reviewing your research plan

- Have you made clear what you plan to do in your study and why? What information do you feel you still need to know?
- Have you identified your study participants and explained why you have chosen them?
- Are the data you have chosen to collect appropriate for your research questions?
- Do you have multiple sources of data?
- Can you explain how each data source will be used to answer each of your research questions?

- If you plan on using interviews or surveys, have you formulated the questions? Do they get at the information you need to answer your research question?

- Have you worked through all the details of your data collection method?

  a. Who will collect the data

  b. In what setting the data will be collected

  c. When and where each type of data will be collected

  d. For how long

- Have you developed an "informed consent" letter that requests permission to use information about study participants, discusses any potential risks to participants, and assures them confidentiality?

- Is your plan for data analysis fully described, including how you will approach your analysis and at what points you will analyze your data?

- Have you identified literature about your question (reference list) that will inform your study?

- Do you have a time line for conducting the study? It should include:

  a. Data collection

  b. Data analysis

  c. Review of literature

  d. Writing a first draft of your findings/conclusion

  e. Revising for the final draft

- Does your research design make sense? Is it credible? Is it plausible?

- What information might still be needed to know?

- How can this plan be enriched or strengthened?

Exercise 6: Planning for a group study with children—clarifying purposes

- What commonalities can you identify among the various questions the children have raised? How can you craft these into an overarching theme that can organize and guide a group study?

- What concepts and content knowledge will this study help students explore, assimilate, and learn how to apply?

- What skills will children acquire or practice during the course of this study?

- What dispositions—attitudes and ways of learning and relating with others—will this study provide opportunities to develop?

Exercise 7: Planning for a group study with children—orchestrating the learning

- What experiences, activities, projects, and experiments will help your students examine the concepts, learn the skills, and develop the dispositions that you intend to nurture?

- How can these learning experiences be sequenced to capitalize on what you know about your students' interests and their current level of skills?

- What kind of activities will be a part of your plan that will utilize many different learning modalities for the diverse learners in your class?

- What out-of-school activities can enrich the learning of the study?

- What cross-grade/age experiences might support the study?

- What activity that is of service to others might be incorporated into this study?

- How can parents/families be involved?

- What homework assignments can support the study?

- What resources—books, materials, technology, etc.—will you need to support the work of this study?

Exercise 8: Planning for a group study with children— reviewing your plans in relation to standards

Use the following grid to review how the plan for your group study addresses required disciplinary content and standards.

Activity	Language arts	Math	Social studies	Science	The arts	Physical education
Activity 1						
Activity 2						
Activity 3						
Activity 4						
Activity 5						
Activity 6						
Activity 7						
Activity 8						
Activity 9						
Activity 10						

- Is there any discipline area or standard that you have not included in your plans?
- If so, are there ways to address what is missing?

*Exercise 9: Planning for a group study with children—
assessing students' progress*

- What ways have you developed to learn about how children's ideas, understandings, and skills are progressing throughout the course of your study?

- How can you use this information to shape your instruction?

- What culminating experience can you develop for the study?

Exercise 10: Personal agendas for children's individual inquiries

Personal Agenda for _____

My inquiry is about: _____

_____

_____

_____

These are the tasks I need to do for my inquiry:

1.

2.

3.

4.

© 2005 by Beverly Falk and Megan Blumenreich from *The Power of Questions* (Portsmouth, NH: Heinemann).

Planning Log for _____

Date	Tasks that I worked on

Data Collection Tools

○ ○ ○

*T*here are many different types of data collection tools that you can use to get evidence to help you answer your research questions. Among these are journals, observations, interviews, surveys, photos, audio/video-tapes, student work samples, and other documents such as teacher or student-kept records. And this is not even an exhaustive list! Teachers are forever finding creative new sources of data. For example, sketches, e-mail conversations, and photographs taken by both teachers and by children are becoming increasingly popular.

As you decide what kinds of data to use, think about how each source will help provide you with answers to your research questions. Also, consider how feasible it will be to collect certain kinds of data within the school day. Sometimes teachers create great research designs and plan to collect amazing amounts of data in diverse and creative ways, but when they actually begin their study, the data collection process feels overwhelming and uncomfortable. Try to select sources that will fit not only your research questions, but also the constraints of the school day and your school life.

A professional journal
Keeping a journal in which you record your thoughts, ideas, questions, or frustrations can be of help to you in the research process. Even though you might think that you will remember a particular moment in your class or an assignment that went well or awry, as time goes on these memories can fade. Especially because completing a research study, collecting all the data, analyzing the data, and writing up the findings takes a considerable amount of time. To keep your memories of significant moments

fresh, you might want to try using a professional journal. In it you may choose to write down realizations about your research topic, reconsiderations of your ideas, an idea of a new method for how to analyze data, or an insight into how to use a particular teaching method in a new way. You can also include reactions to children's responses, experiences such as obtaining permission to interview participants, reactions to your study from co-workers or parents, or information about your relationship with participants outside the regular data collection process.

If you decide to use a journal, do it in a way that best fits your lifestyle. Think about your usual schedule. Are there times during the day when you could faithfully jot down some notes about what has happened during the school day? For instance, many of us take public transportation and use our travel time on the subway or bus to reflect and take notes in a journal. Some teachers spend a few minutes in their classroom at the end of the school day to do the same thing. Another way to journal is to keep a journal file on your computer. Every few days you can jot down some ideas or reflections there.

Field notes

Field notes can take many forms, depending on the overall purpose of your study and your research questions. Field notes of observations in the classroom are a staple of qualitative research methods. They should contain detailed and concrete descriptive information about the setting, the context, and the personal interactions of what/who is being observed (Patton, 1990).

Good field notes (see Figure 6–1) should be dated and include the time, location, and the setting or context in which the observation occurred. They should also use descriptive, rather than evaluative, language. In contrast to evaluative language, which reflects the judgment of the observer, descriptive language focuses on *how* something happens, detailing the process of what happened. It holds the judgment of the observer in abeyance, focusing instead on unpacking the details of what happened in a particular context at a particular time. The following descriptions illustrate the difference. Compare these statements about Andre's progress found in these notes (Falk, 2000)

Andre has an excellent vocabulary.

Andre does outstanding work.

Andre has excellent math skills.

with this version that was completed by Andre's teacher after practicing her observation and documentation skills:

> Andre uses a rich variety of descriptive words in his writing.
>
> Andre works independently and intensely. He thinks critically, takes risks in putting forward new ideas, and is thorough in attention to details of presentation.
>
> Andre is fluid in his thinking about number concepts. He can generally find several solutions to a problem and is able to explain them to others in a clear way.

The second set of descriptions explains what makes Andre's vocabulary and math skills "excellent" and what about his work warrants the characterization of "outstanding." It provides a better picture of *how* Andre does what he does.

Figure 6–1. Characteristics of Good Field Notes

1. Includes the date, place, and setting (the situation/context in which the action occurred)

2. Describes actions of the child/people observed, reactions of other people involved, response of child/people to these reactions

3. Uses descriptive words and phrases and avoids judgmental or evaluative words and phrases (For example, instead of saying that Mario is an excellent writer, describe what Mario does that makes you think that way: Mario's writing is clear, descriptive, well organized, and has a strong sense of voice.)

4. Includes quotes from the child/people observed

5. Supplies "mood cues"—postures, gestures, voice qualities, and facial expressions—that give clues regarding how the child or people being described feel. It does not include interpretations of their feelings.

6. The description is extensive enough to cover the episode. The action or conversation is not left incomplete and unfinished, but is followed through to the point where a little vignette of a behavioral moment is supplied.

Here is an example of a field note entry that is richly descriptive. Notice, additionally, how it provides information about the date, time, and context of the observation.

> Reading: Group, 10/30, 10:00 AM
>
> Context: Teacher chooses a book to read to the entire group at a regular time in the schedule of the day.
>
> Emma is already sitting on the rug. As the teacher sits in front of her preparing to read, Emma slowly turns toward the book although she is very aware of other things in the room and often looks around. She sits on her knees in the general direction of the book without much enthusiasm. She watches the pictures with her finger on her lips. Her interest slightly heightens as her eyebrows raise up and her tongue moves inside her mouth. She hears the other teacher make a noise across the room and glances at her, then back to the book. Her hands move softly around her body and immediate space as she sits, calmly interested. Again Emma shows interest in the book by narrowing her eyebrows and licking her lips at a certain picture. As the teacher asks a general question and looks directly at Emma, she turns slightly crimson, pushes her chin toward her chest, and looks away until the teacher's glance goes elsewhere. Throughout the story, other children asked questions and made comments. Emma remained quiet. When the story was ended the teacher verbally directed the group to the next project. Emma quietly followed the teacher's direction.

When descriptions in this vein accumulate, they paint a rich picture that can help to get the details of the answers to your questions. One primary grade teacher researcher explains how this kind of descriptive data, collected for her inquiry about struggling readers, helped her to understand her students better and to use this information in her instruction (Falk et al., 1995, p. 15).

> Without the written record over time I would miss some kids. Only by looking back over records can you can start to see patterns in what the child is doing—reading, writing— and how it is all connected. All these bits of information

come together into a picture that is particularly useful, especially for kids who are struggling in one way or another. My systematic documentation of children's learning has taught me that whatever conclusions I come to about a child or whatever I am going to try to do next has to be grounded in an observation or a piece of work. Observing children closely generally gives me a lot more than a specific recommendation or a particular method or thing to do for a kid. I walk away with some learning that I can apply to all kids.

Other kinds of field notes that can be collected to aid you in your inquiry are classroom maps, or sketches, that describe the environment. Maps of the classroom can serve multiple purposes. You can use them to study how classroom spaces evolve over the school day or to look at what types of learning or social activities happen in what places and why (Florio–Ruane, 1990). One teacher researcher, Kathryn Zvokel, who was studying DEAR (Drop Everything and Read) time in her classroom, used maps to study the environment of her classroom's library. She made note of how children went about selecting books, made maps of where they went to read them, and took notes on the quality of the experiences in the places where the children read. At the conclusion of her study, Kathryn used what she learned from her notes and her maps to develop a plan for a new library environment. She continued to map her classroom and observe how the changes in environment affected her students' reading experiences.

Observing is complicated work. To organize your thinking during observations, Hubbard and Power (2003) suggest documenting in a double-column notebook, using two thirds of each notebook page for field notes (the actual description of what took place) and one third for "notes on notes" (your reactions to what you documented and/or reflections about it). Other teacher researchers call this activity note taking/ note making (Frank, 1999). Almy and Genishi (1979) suggest yet another way for recording field notes—separating them into three columns: descriptions, feelings, and inferences. The purpose of separating notes in this way is to try to be as objective as possible while recognizing that it is impossible for a teacher simply to observe without having feelings about what he or she is watching (Almy & Genishi, 1979). By separating descriptions from feelings and feelings from inferences, the observer can work to try to use descriptive language that is as objective as possible to describe experiences or behaviors in the classroom, then write down related feelings in a separate section, and then write down conjectures or theories that have emerged during the observation process.

When you are observing, try very hard to record in the description column only your description of what it is the children are doing, not your judgment of their actions. Try to record children's exact words, and when you do, put quotations around them. Then, in the feelings column you can share your feelings about what you saw. Did an action make you feel sympathetic toward the child? Did you find the behavior frustrating? These feelings are important and should be explored throughout your study. In the inference column, should you choose to use one, write about the connections you are making or your questions or thoughts about what you are observing. As you review your notes over time, you may begin to see patterns in your observations that you can interpret or analyze. You can add these in the inferences column along with notes of any anomalies in the behavior or actions that you may notice.

Because at any given time so much can be happening in a classroom, it is easy to lose focus of what you had originally intended to observe. To help you stay focused, before conducting an observation, try to reflect on your purpose for doing it. What type of information do you want to examine? This may help you stay on track and avoid collecting too much extraneous information. Some teacher researchers help anchor their observations by copying the questions for their study in the front of their notebooks. Others try to stay on track by also writing down goals, questions, or techniques they intend to use while observing and putting these in their notebooks as well.

If you are not sure exactly what type of information you are seeking to observe, you might think about conducting observations in phases. The initial phase could involve casting a rather large net, looking at the classroom as a whole. Then, as information that is pertinent to your study emerges, the observations can narrow. The narrowed focus could be on a small group of children who share a quality you wish to study, a particular part of the day, or a certain interaction that you see repeatedly happening throughout the day. The following questions (Boehm & Weinberger, 1997, p. 107) may prove helpful in keeping you focused as you observe:

- What am I trying to sample from the stream of all behavior?
- Why am I interested in the particular information provided by the observation procedures I choose?
- Am I reporting what I see objectively?

- Have unintentional sources of bias been introduced?

- Have I observed long enough and across contexts to obtain a clear picture of the child's behavior?

- Does my recording procedure capture what has happened?

These questions, or others you may create, could also be placed in the front of your observation notebook and could be reviewed, along with your data, from time to time. Regularly reviewing your notes is a good habit to get into, especially right after you have documented them. Doing this will help you to fill in any holes that might have resulted from not having had enough time to write everything down when you were actually taking notes.

A big concern that many teachers have when first starting to make observations is how to manage the task of collecting observations while also juggling the responsibilities of teaching. There are numerous strategies that you can use to do this. Just as students learn differently, teachers also observe and record students' progress in a multitude of ways. Some methods we have observed from teachers we have worked with are the following:

- jotting down observations on note cards

- making notes on computer labels that are carried around on a clipboard and stuck in a folder for a particular child or topic at the end of the day or week

- using sticky notes that get pasted into a notebook at the end of the day

- carrying a notebook that has sections demarcated for each child or topic in which quick notes can be entered during the course of the day and longer reflections noted during preparation periods, lunch, or after-school hours. However you decide to collect observations, if you do it regularly, over time, you will find that you end up with substantial information.

Interviews

The focus of naturalistic, qualitative research is to form deep understandings, to interpret and contextualize experiences (Glesne, 1999). Using interviews as one of your data sources can help you to understand your research participants' perspectives on the matters you are studying. Interviews, because they can be time-consuming, are best suited to finding out in-depth information from a small group of people. If you need to inquire across a large group, surveys or questionnaires (see the following section) are a better data collection choice.

Interviews often happen spontaneously during the course of the data collection process. The contents of such interviews can be documented and used, along with your other data, in your data analysis. However, if you are planning to conduct interviews with several people about the same issue, before doing so it is important to develop an interview guide to ensure that you get consistent information. An interview guide is a list of questions you can use for the interview. When creating this guide, look back at your research questions and consider what type of information you need to answer your research questions at the end of the study.

Interview questions should be open-ended. If you just want a yes or no answer, you can just give out a questionnaire. So remember to frame your interview questions so that they elicit in-depth explanations. Some researchers begin with what is called "grand tour" questions, which are broad and require the participant to give a descriptive answer (Janesick, 1991). Grand tour questions can include asking participants to describe a typical day, to tell you a story about a time when ..., or to share an experience about ....These questions can be followed with smaller "mini-tour" questions related to the same topic, as well as questions that ask for clarification.

Your interview guide should lead you, the interviewer, through a variety of questions that are related to your research topic. However, it should be a flexible document. If during the interview you find that one line of questions is more fruitful than another, you can use your judgment and change your questions accordingly. After the interview, note why and how you changed the interview process, and consider changing the guide in the future. Here is an example of interview questions that Michael asked other teachers in his school for his inquiry about how to create community in the classroom. Note how he kept his question list short so as not to drag out the interview too long and overwhelm the interviewee:

How do you create an environment that makes all children feel that they are part of the group?

How do you gain the trust of your students?

How do you create smooth transitions?

How do you get children to regulate their own behavior?

Some researchers select to interview the same participant several times throughout the data collection period. This is a useful strategy if you want to get a sense of how perceptions of the interviewees progress over time. For example, you might interview some students several times during the school year to get a sense of how their attitudes evolve about a teaching strategy you are trying. In cases such as these, it can be helpful to use data from past interviews as a reference for creating the questions you will use in subsequent interviews. You can ask the interviewees to revisit topics, to speak more about subjects they previously brought up, or to follow up on themes you see emerging during the data collection process.

One key to a good qualitative interview is to imagine the completed transcript (even if you don't intend to transcribe the interview) between you and your interviewee. Who is doing most of the speaking? If the interview transcript is dominated with your talk—your questions and your reactions to the participants' questions—then the interview was probably not as informative as it could be. To accomplish an informative interview you should ask substantial, open-ended questions (which call for long, detailed answers) and then listen carefully to the answers to know how to follow up the questions. Follow-up questions can include asking for more concrete details or for clarification of information that is not clear (see Exercise 3 at the end of the chapter).

Because an interview can yield a lot of information, you might want to consider recording yours. This will give you the opportunity to listen to it after it is done so that you can fully digest what took place and discern details that you might have missed the first time around. Recording your interview can be especially helpful if you want to obtain your interviewee's language verbatim (e.g., for a study of language). Even though you have the tape running, make sure to take notes during the interview so that you can describe body language and other silent cues, as well as ensure you have a record of any words that turn out to be inaudible.

Depending on the goals of your study, you may want to transcribe your interview tapes. You may want to transcribe the entire interview or, after listening to it, you may select to transcribe only what you feel to be relevant pieces of the interview. Or, you could decide to audiotape and only transcribe it if you feel that the notes of the interview were weak in certain crucial areas. If you do decide to transcribe your audiotape, it is best to transcribe the notes the same day or soon after the interview takes place. This will make it easier for you to make sense of what happened because the event will be fresh in your memory.

If you choose to transcribe your audiotape, be aware that it is a time-consuming process. It can take as much as four to five hours to listen to and transcribe one hour of tape. However, the advantage of this method is that, as you go through the process, you begin to analyze and learn more about your data.

Surveys

Surveys or questionnaires are appropriate tools for obtaining information when you want to consult a lot of people. Some researchers choose to begin their studies with a survey to help them select who will meet the criteria they have outlined for their study's participants. Others survey a group to help them select a smaller group of participants that they will interview for a more in-depth phase of data collection. For example, you could survey a large group of people to help you select a smaller group to comprise your study's participants. Or you could survey a large group, all of whom will remain in the study, and then use the information you learned from the survey to select a smaller group that you interview in greater depth.

Surveys can contain close-ended questions, open-ended questions, attitude questions, or a combination of these.

Close-ended questions can be answered with yes or no, true or false, multiple choice answer options, or an attitude (Likert) scale. These kinds of questions are especially useful if one of your research goals is to obtain definitive answers that can be easily aggregated across large groups or expressed as percentages of the whole. For example, if you want to find out how many hours of television are watched, on average, by the children in your class, as part of your study of the impact of television on children's language, or if you want to know the percentage of mothers in your school who work outside the home, then these kinds of questions should be a part of your data collection. Close-ended questions need to be phrased according to the type of answer format you use:

Do you work outside the home? *Circle one:* Yes   No

My child's school is welcoming to parents: *Choose one:* True False

How many hours of television does your child watch each day?

Choose one:

A) 0   B) 1   C) 2   D) 3   E) 4   F) more than 4

I am excited about my inquiry project.

Choose one:

(1) strongly agree   (2) agree   (3) no opinion

(4) disagree   (5) strongly disagree

Open-ended questions, in contrast, are just what their name implies. The degree of the open-endedness of the question allows for greater or lesser variation or interpretation. On one end of the spectrum are fill-in-the-blank questions such as

How many people reside in your household? _____

How old are you? _____

The information provided in the answers to such questions can be graphed or charted but will require additional calculations to produce percentages.

Further along on the spectrum of open-endedness are short-answer questions. These are best asked when seeking information that requires little explanation. Because there can be greater variation among the answers to such questions, these kinds of questions are not as easy to aggregate and are generally asked to get a sense of the range of answers your study participants provide.

What kind of books does your child like to read? _____

What kinds of activities do you and your family do on the weekends? _____

And finally, you can design a survey that asks totally open-ended questions and that provides lots of space for answers. The answers to these, although difficult to aggregate, can give you in-depth information that you can analyze in much the same way that you analyze notes from interviews or observations.

There are a few things to keep in mind when preparing questions for interviews and surveys. One is that the questions in the interview and surveys should not be identical to your research questions. Rather, what you ask should provide information that will get at your research questions in a variety of ways. To help you make sure that your questions are doing this, try making a grid like the one in Figure 6–2 that correlates which questions

Figure 6–2. Correlating Interview and Survey Questions with Research Questions

Research question	Interview question 1	Interview question 2	Interview question 3	Survey question 1	Survey question 2	Survey question 2
#1	X		X			X
#2		X			X	
#3	X			X		

in your interviews and surveys are aimed at answering which one of your research questions. (See Exercise 4 at the end of the chapter.)

Figure 6–3 shows some guidelines to consider when constructing questions for interviews or surveys (Wiersma, 1986).

Documents, work samples, student-kept records, and checklists

Documents, work samples, student-kept records, and checklists can be optimal data sources because they are samples of the real-life work of classrooms and provide an opportunity to study carefully what students are producing in the classroom. They are generally all readily available and fairly easy to collect.

Documents can involve archival data such as past test scores, attendance records, school memos and notices, and communications with caregivers, or "official curriculum" records such as lesson plans and schedules. An example of a study in which you might use documents is one that compares what you actually do in the classroom with what you planned to do. For such a study you could examine and compare lesson plans, schedules, and other forms of the "official curriculum" with your "enacted" curriculum (what actually happens during the school day) (Florio–Ruane, 1990).

Work samples in a range of media from all discipline areas can include copies of students' journals, worksheets, drafts of writing, research projects, portfolios, and other kinds of work from students. These can be used to gather evidence that chronicle progress, uncover the nuances of how students approach their learning, and reveal students' strengths and recurring interests. Writing samples, for example, can reveal much about the nature of individuals' literacy development

- Questions should be clear and unambiguous. Use understandable language. Avoid technical terms, jargon, or vague words.

- Include only one concept in a single question. Do not ask about more than one thing in a question. Do not ask, for example, "Are you in favor of testing and of retaining students who do not pass certain tests?

- Avoid using "leading" questions that imply the answer you are looking for. An example of a leading question is: Do you think children should be tested in kindergarten even though research on child development suggests that testing is not the best way to assess what young children know?

- Avoid questions that elicit responses that might make respondents feel they are inadequate or incapable. An example of such a question might be: Do you have difficulty disciplining your child at home?

- Do not include questions that are outside the realm of what the respondent can answer.

- Make the reading level of the questions appropriate to the respondents.

- Try to get at complex issues through several short questions rather than one long and complex question.

- Ask some questions that require the respondent to answer at length, for instance, "Tell me a story about a time you felt confident with your child's teacher."

- When interviewing young children, you may want to simultaneously play and ask questions which emerge from the play and relate to your study.

- When asking for quantitative information, ask for specifics, not the "average." For example, "How many times last week did you and your child read together?" instead of "On average, how often do you and your child read together?"

- Make answer options cover the full range of answer possibilities, including the option that a person doesn't know or is undecided.

- Avoid asking questions in the negative: Which of the following discipline techniques do you *not* use?

whereas math journals can demonstrate—through algorithms as well as narratives—how students' mathematical thinking is progressing. Research reports, science experiments, projects, drawings, paintings, or other records of artistic endeavors can provide information about students' learning that cuts across disciplines. Photos of three-dimensional work (block buildings, woodworking, experiments, cooking, constructions) and photos of students engaged in activities with others (reading, tending to animals, sports, music, dramatic play) can give a sense of each student's interests and learning styles, and provide information about their learning that is difficult to capture in other ways. Dating these items as they are archived can give a sense of how students progress over time.

In the figures that follow, work samples of Carla, a first grader, demonstrate the progression of her literacy over the course of the school year (Falk, 2000).

The first sample (Figure 6–4) is a piece of Carla's writing, collected during the early months of the school year, which appeared as "scribbles" with accompanying stick figures.

Figure 6–4. Carla's Scribbles

Carla's teacher attached comments to this piece, noting the undeveloped nature of Carla's figure drawings as well as her ability to differentiate between what she considered the print and the pictures.

Another of Carla's work samples (Figure 6–5) from early during the school year is a backward stencil of the alphabet.

Her teacher saved this piece because, to him, it indicated that Carla did not yet fully understand the concept of directionality—that English language print moves from left to right. He noted on the back of the paper that Carla "read" the alphabet to him from right to left.

Several months later Carla's teacher saved a page of words—"cat," "frog," "teddy bear," "inkpad," "stamps," "markers and crayons"—that Carla had copied from classroom charts and labels (see Figure 6–6).

This indicated to him that she was developing a vocabulary of frequently used words and that she was aware of the uses of print in her environment.

Figure 6–5. Carla's Backward Stencil

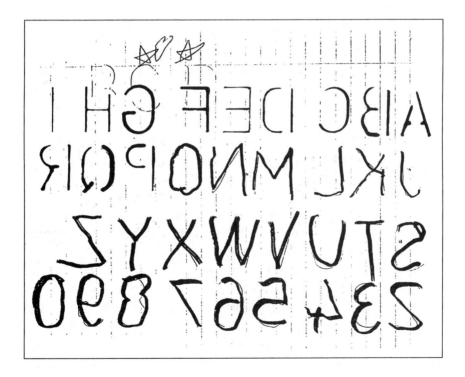

Figure 6–6. Carla's Page of Words

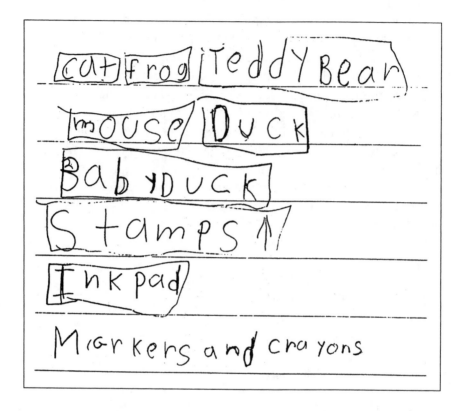

And finally, a writing sample collected during the spring gives evidence of the progress Carla has made (see Figure 6–7). Her pictures are now detailed and include backgrounds for the people.

Her writing, which explains what the picture is about, has progressed to a mix of conventional words along with some phonetic spelling. She demonstrates her sense of the conventions of book language by placing the words "The End" after her written description of the picture.

By systematically collecting these samples of work, Carla's teacher compiled a portrait of her that recorded her developing skills and understandings. Combined with documented observations that he had kept of Carla at work in the classroom, these helped him to note what Carla could do, what she understood, what her interests were, and what skills and understandings he needed to work on with her to enhance her future learning.

Figure 6–7. Carla's Spring Writing Sample

Data Collection
Tools

In much the same way that the mementos in a scrapbook or family album chronicle important lifetime events, collections of student work can provide a record of the evolution of students' developing insights, feelings, understandings, and skills. This kind of information can be used to inform our inquiries, our teaching, and our reports on students' progress, and to make communication with our students and their families more understandable and down to earth (Falk, 2000).

Student-kept records can also be a useful data source for inquiries. These can include reading logs, math journals, notebooks, or project folders. They can chronicle the progress of students' learning and provide information about what students can do and what they understand about important concepts and skills. Even children of the youngest ages can keep records of their reading and writing, their projects, as well as their reflections on their work. These ongoing records can serve not only as data for an inquiry, but can be helpful to the children as well. When students are asked to articulate and keep track of what they have done and what they think, they become more aware of their learning. Student-kept records also help children develop a sense of responsibility, control, and ownership of their work.

Checklists are another form of records that can be completed either by you or your students. You can create and use checklists as a tool to monitor quickly students' behaviors in a variety of ways: to get to know the kinds of choices they make during certain times of the day, to inform discussions you hold at writing conferences, or to assess quickly the students' motivation during different activities. Students too can use them to evaluate their participation in groups, their feelings about different aspects of a project, or to assess their own work.

Audiotapes/videotapes

Audiotapes and videotapes can be helpful ways to document what takes place in your classroom. (Before taping, always make sure to obtain permission from the people you intend to tape.) If recorders are placed in the midst of students at work, they can be especially helpful for studying what goes on without influencing the data through your presence. For example, some teachers place tape recorders with cooperative groups or in centers in their classroom to hear how children work through certain problems on their own.

Videotape can be particularly useful to help you understand how people interact, how they use body language, what is happening in conversations between multiple participants or focus groups, or how a particular strategy actually works in the classroom. Most teachers find that their students become comfortable around audio- and videotapes in a relatively short time and are not inhibited by the taping process.

Videotapes can also be used for self-examination and analysis. Teachers can use videos to examine themselves while teaching. Students can use videos to analyze their own actions in the classroom. Think back to the earlier example of Ryan's study when he had his students analyze their input while in literature circles. He videotaped his students in literature groups and asked them to analyze the tape with him. He and his students then used these tapes to develop criteria for effective conversations.

Data collection concerns

If you are new to collecting data, you may have many questions about how to go about the task. One question you may have is how much data you should collect. There is no right answer to this question. The amount of data that is just right is highly individualized and dependent on the particulars of your study. However, a few general guidelines are that too much data will make you feel like you are drowning and may be too much to process realistically; too little data will not give you sufficient information to answer your research questions. The "right" amount for you should provide you with enough evidence to identify recurring themes, let you know if you need to adjust your study, help you think about your research questions in new ways, and reveal insights that were not initially clear when you first designed your study. To help you figure out the amount of data that will be best for your study, try imagining, before you begin your data collection, what it will take to collect all the data that you have proposed to collect.

Getting as specific as possible will also help you to make realistic plans. As you think about the types of data you will use, consider exactly how you intend to use them. What questions will you ask? How will you focus your observations? How much time will be needed to achieve the information you are striving for?

You may also be wondering about the number of data sources you need. As noted earlier, in teacher inquiry it is important to select several data sources to triangulate data to ensure the validity of your study. Studies that rely on just one data collection technique can present a skewed or limited impression of what actually is happening during the study (Patton, 1990). For example, consider studying the effectiveness of a particular teaching strategy. One data source could involve interviewing a child about how the strategy felt to him or her. Did the strategy help him or her learn? The child may enthusiastically reply that the strategy really did help. This is useful information in terms of understanding the child's perspective and perhaps also his or her motivation to learn. However, if the focus of the study is to understand the effectiveness of the teaching strategy, additional data sources would be needed. Observations of children using the strategy, and children's work samples and test scores would provide a more complete understanding of the impact of the strategy in the context of the classroom.

As you begin to collect data for your study, you may feel overwhelmed by what seems like the enormity of the task. You may feel that such record keeping takes too much time and that it would be much easier and less time-consuming just to keep track of this information in your memory. However, as you gain experience documenting observations and collecting data—from a variety of settings in a variety of ways—you will most likely find, like we have, that you are learning more from this process than you had ever imagined was possible. Over time you will learn how to fit data collection, such as keeping field notes, into the cracks of your teaching day. You can develop regular times when you take notes, such as while students are working in groups or working independently. You can incorporate a regular time to collect or make copies of student work. From these activities you may find that you are seeing so many things that you had not noticed before that you may make jotting down, collecting, and reflecting a part of your "teacherly" way of life (Falk, 2000).

Data resources for children's research

There are many resources that children can use to carry out research. Because children, especially young children, learn through active exploration, social interaction, and guidance from adults, it is important, in addition to books, that they have classrooms set up with a variety of materials, that they have lots of opportunities to interact with them, and that they are exposed to a broad range of experiences with many different people, places, and things. Additionally, it is important that, while children are engaged with these materials and experiences, they also are able to talk, share, debate, and work together. The data sources for children's inquiries thus should include observations and experimentation with plants, animals, water tables, bulbs, batteries, cooking ingredients, blocks, materials for art, mathematics, science, and others. Trips, interviews, print and media materials such as newspapers, magazines, the Internet, TV, and of course other classmates can also be rich sources of data (see Exercise 5 at the end of the chapter).

Data sources for a study of the civil rights movement could be, in addition to literature and archival information, a trip to a center for African American literature and culture, and a showing of one of the numerous plays or movies made about that time. For a study of architecture, a tour of buildings would be an appropriate data source. Children could also take photographs, draw pictures, learn about drafting, and interview architects. For a study of immigration, different ethnic neighborhoods could be visited. Additionally, children could develop interview questions and interview recent immigrants, and study their own family's history of immigration by collecting artifacts from home (such as photographs, stamps and coins, a family tree, dolls or other ethnic artwork).

As children proceed through their inquiries, whether individually or as a group, it is essential to keep track of their progress so that the next steps for their investigations can be supported. Regular review of children's work and record keeping of their developing knowledge and skills provide insights to what they know, what they understand, and what questions they are developing. Some teachers use reflection sheets at the close of class work sessions that ask questions such as the following:

What did you work on today?

While working, what did you notice about what you were doing?

What problems did you have? Or where did you get stuck?

What questions do you still have that you want to explore?
(Falk & Margolin, 2005)

Folders allocated for project work can be used to keep track of what students do during classroom time (see the discussion of these in the last chapter). In them the children can record their questions, how they arose, how they proceeded to answer them, and what they learned about them through their investigations.

Providing time for students to share these work records with their classmates can also be valuable. The discussions that ensue from this type of sharing can help students to clarify their thinking. In addition, such conversations can stimulate new directions that can deepen and extend individual or group work. Take, for example, teacher Susan Gordon's fifth grade class' study of flight (Falk, 2000), discussed in more detail in Chapter 9. Initiated by a trip to an aeronautics museum, the flight curriculum engaged students in experiences that involved literacy, math, science, and social studies. For this study, all students were required to complete a common set of activities. In addition, each student was challenged to pursue one aspect of the study independently and in depth. Some created airplane designs and then built models of them. Some did research on aviation history. Some read the biographies of famous pilots. At regular intervals Susan led the class in a discussion of their project work, inviting different students to share the progress of their projects with the other students in the class. This inevitably led to new questions for the presenters, raised by others in the class, which provided directions for further study.

Ongoing records of work kept by children can be shared at class meetings, making it possible for the whole group to develop a common body of knowledge without everyone having to do the same thing at the same time. Group discussions of works-in-progress can provide each individual with guidance for their studies as well as exposure to a wider world of information and ideas than any one individual could get from pursuing a study alone.

Group learning can be further enhanced by keeping a record of class discussions on large chart paper and displaying it sequentially on classroom walls. This documentation provides a chronicle of the classroom as a learning community that all members can use as a reference and reminder over time (Falk, 2000). The Reggio Emilia schools in northern Italy have publicized this way of documenting the learning journey of a whole class. Recording class learning in this way enables discussion to elevate to deeper discourse, group remembering to support revisiting of powerful ideas, symbols to turn into languages of learning, listening to include hearing others' meanings, understanding to lead to provocation of new ideas, encounters to expand into projects, community involvement to develop into partnerships, and assessment to become rich inquiry (Edwards et al., 1998).

Exercise 1: Sharpening your observation tools

Being a careful observer is a vital research tool. In this exercise, practice observing with a photograph of a classroom event.

- Divide a piece of paper into two columns: Notes (descriptions) and Notes on Notes (interpretations, assumptions, judgments) (Hubbard & Power, 2003).

- As you look at the picture, write down everything you see happening in the Notes section. Be descriptive. Do not make assumptions or inferences. Only describe what you see.

- Then, in the Notes on Notes section, write down any assumptions, questions, or feelings you may have about what you see.

Share your Notes and Notes on Notes with a colleague. Ask yourselves the following:

- How do you know what you have put in the Notes section?

- Is there evidence for what you have written or have you inferred it?

For example, if a child is sitting next to another child with a book in front of them, don't assume that one is tutoring the other, that they are happy if they have smiles on their faces, or that they are working quietly. Just describe it as you see it. In the Notes sections you might write: Two girls are sitting next to each other at a table. An open book is on the table. The girls are smiling. In the Notes on Notes column you might write: Are they engaged in pair–share reading? Are they having a good time? Is one tutoring the other?

Exercise 2: Inquiry tools

Try out each of the following inquiry tools:

- Journal: Keep a journal for a week to reflect on your thoughts while teaching.

- Observations: Try documenting several observations of a child and of classroom events in a double- or triple-column notebook. Make sure you are descriptive and keep your reactions, feelings, judgments, and inferences out of the description section.

- Documents, work samples, checklists: Collect a range of evidence about one student. Describe what each piece of evidence demonstrates.

- Student records: Ask your students to keep track of their learning in either a log of their readings, a writer's notebook, a math journal, etc. Review these materials to get a better sense of how your students are thinking, understanding, and processing their work.

- Interviews: Prepare interview questions about a question or issue of concern to you. Try these interview questions on someone to see how much information you get from the questions you have asked.

- Surveys: Draft a survey or questionnaire related to a question you have. Try the survey out on a few people to see if it gives you information that will help answer your research question.

- Audio- or videotapes: Try recording a classroom conversation and/or videographing you and your class. Review the tape to see what it reveals. Try transcribing a small section to get a sense of what you can learn from the process.

Exercise 3: Peer editing—developing interview questions

Write some questions you would like to ask your study's participants. Go over the interview questions yourself or ask a critical friend to review them in relation to the following:

- Are these questions related to your research questions? Will they help you to find out information you will need to answer your research questions?
- Are these questions open-ended?
- Do any of the questions carry assumptions?
- Do you have a variety of types of questions—grand tour, mini tour, follow-up, etc.?
- Are the questions clear?

Exercise 4: Correlating your interview or survey questions to your research questions

Create a chart like the one in Figure 6–2 to correlate the questions in your interviews and surveys with your research questions.

Exercise 5: Eliciting data sources from children

Hold a class discussion about what sources of information to seek to enhance, enrich, or extend whatever you are currently studying. Chart the answers the children provide and try one of their suggestions. After charting the answers the children provide, evaluate the different data sources with the children. Are they all equally valuable? Are some sources more feasible to collect than others? Ask the students to consider how exactly they could collect the data. Assign the children to collect data either individually or in small groups as you feel fits the project best.

Making Sense of Your Learnings
Analyzing Data

● ● ●

*A*nalyzing your data is an ongoing process that begins as soon as you start collecting it. Each time you collect data you should try to make time to review what you have and reflect on it. Sometimes this initial data analysis will take the form of jotting down your thoughts about what you have collected in the margins of your field notes, journal, interview transcripts, or survey forms. Sometimes it will be giving a name to an idea or theme that you see recurring in these various forms of evidence. Only through this ongoing regular review—also referred to as *formative analysis*—will you avoid becoming overwhelmed by the data you are collecting. It's just like keeping your desk neat. If you wait until everything piles up too high, the task of cleaning seems impossible. If you regularly organize what you use, you can easily and painlessly stay on top of your work.

Besides keeping you from getting overwhelmed, ongoing, regular analysis will provide you with understandings that will assist you in moving forward with your study. As you read through your notes, you may find new insights, directions, or questions arising that will point you toward areas that you need to explore further. For example, you might begin to see a theme emerging from your note taking in the classroom that will make you more aware of other situations that fit into that theme. This happened for one teacher when she reviewed her classroom notes taken as part of her study on "What are effective teaching strategies for children in diverse urban classrooms?" Her notes were filled with examples of how she wove skill work into the context of interesting, engaging content and activities. Before reviewing her notes, she had not been aware that this was what she was doing. After recognizing this strategy in her data, she began more consciously to examine how she did it. As a result, she not only discovered many elements of her teaching that she had not been aware of before, she also gained insight into how she used them effectively.

Another benefit of ongoing, regular data review is that you might find, when reviewing the data, that while you are getting lots of evidence, most of it pertains to only two of your three research subquestions. Discovering this before you have finished collecting your data will allow you to make a conscious effort in your subsequent observations to look specifically for the missing information. This conscious look for the missing data may lead you to see things you have not perceived before.

Finally, regular review of your data may help you to develop hunches about what you are seeing or learning. You might want to keep a notebook or file on your computer of "Memos to Myself," where you can make note of your ideas throughout the data collection period.

Organizing your evidence into themes or categories

Once you have finished collecting your data, you begin a different stage of data analysis—organizing your evidence into themes or categories that will help you make sense of it so that you will eventually come up with a set of findings.

In your research plan you decided how you would analyze your data. Begin by rereading that plan and carefully examining the data you collected. It's likely that you will have to review your data several times before you can see the big picture that it is giving you. After you do this you will need to ask yourself if your original plan still makes sense. If you decide to change your analysis plan at any point, be sure to make note of why you are making this change so that you can explain it in your final report.

There are different ways to arrive at your themes or categories. Just remember, as you go about your analysis, that just as there is no "right" question or answer in research, there is no "right" analysis either. As long as research methods are valid, data can be interpreted in a variety of ways. What makes it all work is if the research plan is coherent, the findings are supported by evidence, and the analysis of the findings makes sense. In the following sections we describe and explain two approaches to data analysis: a priori and emergent analysis.

Analysis using a priori themes ○ This method of analysis utilizes pre-determined themes or categories to sort the data you have collected throughout your study. These themes, most probably, are the areas of inquiry around which you have built your research subquestions. For example, if you are examining the impact of play on the young child, your subquestions may have been constructed to look for the impact of play on (1) cognitive development, (2) social/emotional development, and (3) physical development. These are the themes or categories you will look for as you review your data.

Or, you could be doing a study that examines your classroom for how well it supports various aspects of children's development. Your subquestions for this inquiry might be how the classroom facilitates children's (1) physical development, (2) cognitive development, (3) language development, (4) relations with peers, (5) relations with adults, (6) interests, and (7) imagination and creativity. Here again, the categories or themes you are looking for are defined by your research subquestions.

Analysis using emergent themes ○ Sometimes, however, even when your research subquestions are clearly defined and you are organizing your data around them, you may find evidence that just doesn't seem to fit in any category. Such "emergent" themes should definitely be utilized in your analysis. A case in point might be the study of the impact of play on young children referred to earlier. When teacher researcher Nereida Saban did this study and was sorting through her data, she found, in addition to the originally defined themes of cognitive, social/emotional, and physical development, that there were a lot of incidences during which gender was affecting how children played. So she added the category of gender to her analysis and sorted all the evidence that had to do with gender into it.

Emergent themes can also be the way in which your entire analysis flows. In this case, your research question and subquestions may only be a starting point for your inquiry. As you investigate, the answers to your questions emerge in a different form than the way you framed the questions. Understandings and theories may emerge from the data. Sometimes this approach is called *grounded theory* (Glaser & Strauss, 1967).

Sheri's study of what American math teachers can learn from Japanese math teaching methods and professional development is an

example of an emergent theme analysis. She began her study with the
following subquestions:

- How are specific math problems approached in Japanese classrooms?

- How do Japanese math teachers view problem solving?

- How can American classrooms that are moving toward a more Japanese-style deductive approach to mathematics handle problem solving?

- How can American educators incorporate the Japanese professional development practice of Lesson Study into their own teaching practices?

Her findings were organized around the following themes:

- In Japan, everything revolves around how students think.

- Both Japanese students and teachers learn to think mathematically through an investigation and exploration process.

- Allow students to investigate mathematical concepts on their own.

- American teachers need to ask students "why" and "how" questions.

- American teachers need to plan in a collaborative setting.

- American teachers need to explore how students think.

- Teachers need to focus on multiple solutions in the classroom.

Whichever way your analysis develops, we offer in the following part of this chapter, suggestions about how to negotiate the process.

Getting started: The first sifts, shakes, and shuffles

One way to help you get started with the organization of your data and its analysis is to write yourself an "analysis memo." Reflect on what you have seen, heard, and collected, and do a free write about what you think you are finding. This process can help you to begin identifying your themes, both the categories you originally specified in your research subquestions as well as those that might have appeared unexpectedly. This will help you get a tentative sense of what you are looking for. Then, as you sort through your data, you can test your themes to see if they are supported by evidence (see Exercise 1 at the end of the chapter).

Or, another way to get started with your analysis is to take some time "playing" with the data. This activity can take different forms. You can read through the data and start making piles of materials that seem to work together. You can write notes about your notes. You can develop index cards that describe the important themes in your study. You can look through your data to identify what doesn't fit. You can make copies of your data and then cut up examples and sort them in different ways. You can draw a picture of a metaphor that seems to represent what you are seeing. Or you can pull out stories that seem to resonate to you. Be as creative or as linear as you like. Examine the data in a way that is in line with your own learning strengths. After this play time, you will be ready for a more systematic approach (see Exercise 2 at the end of the chapter).

Coding your data

To ensure that the findings you eventually arrive at are based on evidence, not just your perceptions, feelings, or thoughts, you need to have a systematic process for sorting your data in themes or categories. One of the most effective ways to do this is to "code" it. Colored pencils or highlight pens are helpful coding tools. With them you can assign a color to each designated or emergent theme.

To code your data, read through your field notes, interview questions, survey questions, or reflective journal. Then highlight with the designated colors the words that give you information about the themes of your subquestions or the themes that emerge. You will need to go through your data several times to get the coding of your data right. You may find, for example, after the first round of coding, that when you review it again, you realize that the code you originally selected does not quite describe the information you collected. Change and/or adapt your codes as you go along. Most likely, it will take several readings to make sure that you are categorizing all the information you have (see Exercise 4 at the end of the chapter). Below are two observations, documented by teacher researcher Allison, of Emma, a two-year-old she was observing for her study. She coded them to the emergent themes of relations with adults, relations with peers, interest in literacy, sense of self, and language development.

○ *Observation #1*

Reading: Group, 10/30, 10:00 AM

Context: Teacher chooses a book to read to the entire group at a regular time in the schedule of the day.

Emma is already sitting on the rug. As the teacher sits in front of her preparing to read, Emma slowly turns toward the book although she is very aware of other things in the room and often looks around. She sits on her knees in the general direction of the book without much enthusiasm. She watches the pictures with her finger on her lips. Her interest slightly heightens as her eyebrows rise up and her tongue moves inside her mouth. She hears the other teacher make a noise across the room and glances at her, then back to the book. Her hands move softly around her body and immediate space as she sits, calmly interested. Again Emma shows interest in the book by narrowing her eyebrows and licking her lips at a certain picture. As the teacher asks a general question and looks directly at Emma, she turns slightly crimson, pushes her chin toward her chest, and looks away until the teacher's glance goes elsewhere. Throughout the story, other children asked questions and made comments. Emma remained quiet. When the story was ended the teacher verbally directed the group to the next project. Emma quietly followed the teacher's direction.

○ Observation #2

Reading: One on one, 10/30, 10:45 AM

Context: During snack time I asked Emma if she would read a book with me when she finished. She nodded her head.

After snack time, Emma and I went to the bookcase. Emma looked in many books before she decided on the airport book. She allowed herself to be put on my lap. As soon as we opened the book, Emma burst out with language. She pointed to different planes and commented on the color correctly. She told me in which plane she was going and with whom, "MOMMY." She answered questions about the pictures, often elaborating her answers with stories of her own experience. (She recently returned from a vacation where she took a plane.) She told the story from the pictures with gusto, using words, expressions, and gestures as she "read" the story and told her own. We needed to stop reading abruptly to make a jack-o-lantern. After the activity, Emma did not want to return to the book immediately, but instead played with the toy people for a while. I placed the book on a bench, open to the page we left off. After a few minutes, Emma picked up the book, came to me, and resumed "reading" the book through its pictures. "We fly through the sky," she exclaimed as she pointed up to the ceiling. "Look at it," she said to a classmate, pointing to the picture. After we read the book once together, Emma sat away from me, book in tow, and "read" it once again by herself. She turned each page one by one, commenting the whole way through about her own airplane trip. After she was satisfied with the book, she left it and went to play with the dolls. However, she remained very possessive of it throughout the day, grabbing it from others who picked it up, yelling with a whine "noooo." She needed assistance to look at the book together with another child and to allow others a turn.

As you can see from these two documentations, Emma acted very differently in the two different contexts. If Allison had not had both observations to reference, she might have drawn very different conclusions about several of the themes that were guiding her analysis. Try analyzing Emma's behavior and how it fits into the themes Allison developed in Exercise 3 at the end of the chapter.

Triangulating data

A careful review of Allison's data reveals why it is essential to have multiple forms of evidence (triangulated data) to substantiate your themes or categories. One observation or one piece of evidence may not be representative of the trend that numerous observations or pieces of evidence might reveal. For example, during the first documented observation of Emma during a group reading activity, she appears to be uninterested in listening to the story being read by the teacher, has difficulty focusing, expresses herself minimally, and is shy and fearful of adults. However, the second observation of Emma in a one-to-one encounter with an adult offers a view with very different traits. Given the opportunity to choose her own text, she is interested and focused, verbal and expressive about her ideas, quite comfortable with the adult, and interested in engaging with other children.

If only one of these documented observations were read, a reader might get an inaccurate and incomplete impression of Emma. This is why, in qualitative research, trends and themes need to be confirmed in more than one data source to ensure that the findings of a study are not merely happenstance.

Ethics and bias

In Chapter 5 we discussed consent forms and the importance of obtaining permission to conduct a study. Involving study participants in the data analysis process is another way to protect them. Many researchers believe that the process between the researcher and the study participants should be "dialogical" (i.e., informed by each other's thinking) (Tierney, 1993). When this is done, the researcher and the "researched" are often said to have created a "shared understanding" (Hatch & Wisniewski, 1995). In fact, some even believe that if the subjects of the research are excluded from the construction of the final findings, the result silences those to whom it purports to give voice.

It is important to remember that a study written by one researcher is always the researcher's construction of reality. Even if the researcher aims to share as much raw data as possible or the participants' voices verbatim, the researcher's views subtly dominate the study. This is because the researcher is the one who chooses the questions to ask and decides what data to include in the findings. All this cannot help but affect the final results of the study. One way to work toward ensuring that the participants' point of view is depicted as authentically as possible is to ask participants to take part in "member checks" that involve helping to analyze the data and/or reading the drafts of the findings of the data analysis.

Peer work: Ensuring reliability of your coding

A "member check" for data analysis involves checking your coding with your study's participants to ensure that you are organizing your data around themes that reflect everyone's perspectives and that make sense. You can also check your analysis with a friend or colleague to see if your analysis is "reliable" (i.e., is reflecting what the data show). Doing such a check will reassure you and the readers of your study that your method of coding is sound. The way to do a reliability check is to have someone review a part of your data, looking for evidence that fits under the themes or categories you have decided on. You provide the colleague with the themes, but you must not reveal to your colleague how you have coded it. The goal is for you both to come up with similar judgments about categorizing the evidence. You do not have to do a formal statistical analysis of the percentage of agreement in the coding between you and your colleague, but you do want to achieve substantial agreement, in the ballpark of at least eighty percent.

When doing your reliability check with your partner, whenever there is disagreement in your judgments you should discuss each instance about which you disagree, using the evidence to argue about to which category it should belong. By doing this, you will gain a better understanding of your themes and what evidence supports them. This will lead you both to greater consensus and thus more reliable judgments about them. If you had a lot of disagreements the first time around, try repeating the reliability check with another piece of data. After you have reached consensus several times on the coding you review, you will have greater assurance that it is reliable and thus the validity of your study will be strengthened (see Exercise 5 at the end of the chapter).

Not all studies are suitable for this type of analysis. For instance, if you are conducting a study about your own perception of a phenomenon in your classroom, how others interpret your data is not as important as your own analysis and construction of the findings. As with each part of your study, you will have to select and defend the methodologies you use based on your goals and your research questions.

Reflective analysis

In addition to coding your data, another analysis process you can make use of is your own reflections about your data. As you read and categorize your notes, interviews, and surveys, your review will undoubtedly trigger new thoughts about what you saw or heard or received. Make sure that you jot these down. Sometimes your notes will be about your themes. Sometimes they will be about questions you have. Sometimes they may even be notations about your research method. This process of questioning, putting a name to something you are seeing in the data, reminding yourself about an idea or issue, is all part of the analytical process. Each time you do it you will arrive at a deeper stage of understanding.

This kind of reflective analysis works well for reviewing samples of work, photographs, or other records you might have collected. As you analyze these materials you will be able to determine which artifacts you have collected that will help you answer your research questions and which don't pertain. To help you determine what is useful, try asking some of the questions in Figure 7–1 (Falk, 2000) (see Exercise 6 at the end of the chapter).

One way to help you keep track of the documents you are collecting is to number each work sample (WS 1, WS 2) and photo (P1, P2) and then use sticky notes to jot down what you see in each piece of evidence. For example, if your study is about how you can help to support children's reading through their writing, you are probably collecting writing samples. You might make note of what each piece of writing reveals to you about the child's reading progress (see Figures 6–4 through 6–7 in Chapter 6).

Data analysis chart

To help you make sense of your analyzed artifacts and coded data, making a chart of your findings can be helpful. A chart that organizes these

Figure 7–1. Questions for Looking at Student Work

1. What was the context in which the work was created?

2. What questions does this work raise about the student (i.e., the student's intent or interests)?

3. What does this work demonstrate about what the student understands, what the student can do, and how the student meets standards/expectations for the work?

4. What does this work demonstrate about the student's growth over time?

5. What does this work tell about the instruction and learning environment that prompted the work? How effective were the assignment and teaching strategies?

6. What does this work suggest about the kind of teaching and opportunities for learning that should come next for this student?

findings into your themes or subquestions will make it possible for you to see clearly in one place all the evidence for each category. Here is an outline of an analysis chart, using themes from Nereida's study on play:

Data source	Theme #1: Academic development (yellow)	Theme #2 Social/ development (green)	Theme #3 Physical development (blue)	Theme #4 Gender differences (pink)	Emergent Theme (orange)
Observations					
Student work samples					
Reflective journal					
Photographs					

You can use this chart (see Exercise 7 at the end of the chapter) by substituting your themes in the top row and, in the appropriate column allocated to each theme, by categorizing the highlighted sections of your observations, quotes, photos, or work samples. Type up the evidence that you highlighted for each theme as you sifted through your data and then put it in the appropriate column. Then put all the highlighted sections in the row of the data source from which it came. The final column is for interesting outliers or emergent themes. Note pieces of your data that may not be representative, but that seem important to you for other reasons. Later you can decide if these or other pieces on the chart merit inclusion in your research findings. You should also include any notes you have made (the preliminary analysis)—your ideas, reflections, or questions—about your observations, interviews, surveys, work samples, photos, or other documents. Organizing your data in this way will make it easier when you begin writing up your findings because your evidence will already be transcribed and arranged by theme, ready to be referenced to support your assertions.

On the following page is an excerpted data analysis chart from Natalie's study of how to support students' independent learning at center time in kindergarten. This chart lists relevant observations under the themes (derived from subquestions) of her study.

Children as their own teachers	Play in centers impacting development	How anecdotals drive teaching	Extensions of mini lessons in play
1/27: Reader's Workshop Center: Watching the children figure out a new center activity— using a mini stapler and making a flip book. One of them took charge and showed them all how to use it. *2/23: Independent Reading Time:* Aryana is looking over Jed's shoulder as he is reading. She is encouraging him and talking about the book.	*2/5: Kitchen Center:* Leila is in the stroller crying like a baby. The other girl and boy in the kitchen were comforting her. *3/9: Block Center:* The children put the blocks away, stacking them according to size and shape.	*1/26: Note to myself:* The children had expressed an interest in the sequence of a story. So I made a paper with three boxes so they could experiment with sequencing in their own writing. *2/06: Writing Center:* As I saw the kids confuse and try to write and even say the blends of "ch" and "sh" and the word endings "ing" and "ed," I decided to begin doing mini lessons on them during phonics.	*1/20: Reader's Workshop Center:* After Guided Reading Group, Maya and Soo-ling are writing/drawing with colored pencils and markers. They are writing words "this" and "family" from the books we just read (*I Love My Family* and *Our Families*). *1/27: Writing Center:* After a mini lesson on word endings, James is writing sentences. He is writing "playing" and he is saying "ing" over and over in his head and out loud. He finally writes "ing."

Indexing

Another way to chart the themes of your data is to make an index chart. Instead of analyzing your data by including it word for word in a chart, an index allows you to see what type and how much data you have to support your themes, or the developing findings, at a glance. To index your data you need to go through your observational journal and number each page. You need to do the same with your interview notes, your surveys, and your work samples, photos, or other documents. Everything should be numbered. The notes can be labeled N (for notes) 1, N2, N3, etc. The interviews can be numbered I1, I2, I3, etc. Use S for surveys, WS for work samples, P for photos, etc. Then number each highlighted mark for each specific form of evidence so that it can be easily identified on the page. For example, if you have three yellow highlights on page 1 of your notes, they would be numbered page N1.1, N1.2, and N1.3. For an index chart, instead of rewriting all the words from each highlighted section of your notes, you can simply reference each excerpt with its number in each column and row of the chart. Here is an example of part of an index from a narrative study of an eight-year-old boy with a chronic illness:

Index Chart "Matthew"

Category	Pages
Relationship with mother	I13–16, I41, I45, WS5, N31–32,
Religion	I50, I61, N13, N20
Father	I17
Medicine	I30–31, N15–16, P2
Teacher	I5–7, I50–52, I72, WS3, WS4, N5–10, N38
Brothers and sisters	I2, I12, I28, N12, N20
Uniform	I13, I21
Field trips	I24, I71, WS7, WS8

Developing a working outline

One additional strategy you can use to analyze your data, with or without using a data analysis or index chart, is to create a working outline of your findings. Each theme can be considered a tentative finding. Go through your data, find examples that support each of the themes, and count how many times you see evidence of each theme. Get rid of themes that are not supported with ample data or that do not seem significant after careful study. Continue to revise the outline until you feel it is a good representation of the data you have collected (see Exercise 8 at the end of the chapter).

Taking the process "bird by bird"

Utilizing these data analysis methods should make the data analysis process more manageable. However, if you are feeling overwhelmed, try to stay focused and take it one step at a time. Think of this story by Anne Lamott from her book *Bird by Bird: Some Instructions on Writing and Life* (1994) in which she recounts a scene from her childhood, one late Sunday night, when her brother sat at the kitchen table with books spread out, holding his head in his hands, paralyzed by the task of completing a report on birds that was due the very next day. Although it had been assigned many weeks before, he had procrastinated and was now freaked out by the enormity of what he had to do. Their father came into the room, put his arm around the child's shoulders, and said in a calm steady voice, "Take it bird by bird, my son. It is the only way to get through."

Remember to take it "bird by bird" as you go through the data analysis process. If you do, you will find yourself soon ready to write up your findings.

Helping children analyze their data

The same processes you use for data analysis can be used with your students in a simplified form (see the exercises at the end of the chapter). For students' individual studies, you may want to begin by orchestrating some "play" time with the data. Some activities they can try include sorting through their data several times and then drawing a picture that represents what they are seeing. They can also put their working themes on index cards and then note some examples of each theme. Or they can share what they believe are important themes with a partner and then give each other several examples for each theme.

When it is time for students to look through the data more systematically, coding data is probably too complex, but charts can be useful in helping children organize their ideas and understandings. As they look through the data they collect, they can create a column for each research subquestion and put all the information for each question in the appropriate column. Retyping the information on the computer will make it easier to use later when they are writing up findings. This step will also help ease the process of making sense of what they have read or collected. The chart can have rows that further organize the data by source—readings, interviews, surveys, etc. This will help students remember from which source the information came. Later, when they are writing about their findings, this reference information will be important, because they need to learn to cite where information comes from.

Figure 7–2. Children's Data Analysis Chart

Data source	Theme #1:	Theme #2:	Theme #3:	Theme #4:
Observations				
Readings				
Reflective journal				
Surveys				

Data analysis is an activity ripe with potential for learning. Depending on the age group of your students and your own teaching goals, you can use data analysis as a sorting activity or as an introduction to outlining, developing a persuasive argument, or evaluating. For instance, after creating charts with your students, you can teach them how to evaluate the themes and how to decide what is a worthwhile finding to share. The students could work with you to develop criteria for a good finding, or you could provide criteria for them. (Examples of criteria for a good research finding may include having ample examples and evidence to support the theme, answering all aspects of the research questions, or providing convincing information.) If skill work like this is done in the context of studies based on students' burning questions, it can become a vital learning experience rather than simply a routine exercise.

For group studies, the class charting described at the end of Chapter 6 can be a helpful way to analyze learnings. At class meetings you can record students' developing understandings on charts and regularly have discussions that further probe and prod their thinking. The charts can be displayed on the classroom walls so that all can see how their ideas are advancing. This documentation can be referred to regularly and transferred to an analysis chart at the conclusion of the study.

Exercise 1: Writing an analysis memo

Write a memo to yourself about the data you have been collecting. Reflect on what you have seen and heard, and free write about what you think you are finding. What are some of the themes you are finding?

Exercise 2: Playing with your data

Make copies of your notes and other data either on paper or on the computer. Sift through the materials and start making piles that seem to work together. Write notes to yourself about what you have collected. On index cards, write down what you think are the important themes of your study. Now look through all your data again and see what data seem not to fit Try sorting it in different ways.

Exercise 3: Coding the observations of Emma

Review the two earlier observations of Emma. Code them for the following themes: relations with adults, relations with peers, interest in literacy, sense of self, and language development. What are the differences you find between the two observations?

Exercise 4: Coding your own data

Try coding your own data:

- Begin by assigning a separate colored pencil or highlight pen to each a priori theme or research subquestion.

- As you read through your data, each time you find something that provides information that can help you answer one of your research subquestions, highlight it with the color you have assigned to that question or theme.

- At the same time, take notes of emerging themes. As you feel more confident about these themes, assign them a color and reread your data highlighting these themes.

- Assess your themes when you are done coding:

  - Are there themes with little evidence? If so, you may choose to eliminate the theme.

  - Are there themes that need to be renamed?

  - Can you conflate some of the themes into one theme?

Exercise 5: Conducting a member check

- Ask a colleague to review some of your data and code it according to themes. Provide the colleague with the themes you have chosen for your analysis.

- Review how your colleague's coding compares with yours.

- In places where you disagree, discuss the differences using the evidence to support your judgments.

- Repeat this process with other data excerpts until you have agreed on your coding a few times.

Exercise 6: Looking at student work

Review some samples of student work with the questions in Figure 7–1.

Exercise 7: Charting your developing findings

After your data have been coded, chart the findings for each theme or subquestion to see clearly in one place all the evidence for each category.

- Make a chart like the one that follows.

- Write the data sources you are using down the left column and write each theme or emerging theme across the top.

- Include a column for interesting outliers (other themes that emerge) as well. This will give you a place for data that seems significant but does not fit into your themes.

- Fill in the chart with the actual data or fill it in with references to the data as in the index chart described earlier.

Exercise 8: Making an outline

- List the themes in your data.

- Cite examples that support each of the themes.

- Count how many times you saw evidence of the theme.

- Get rid of themes that are not supported by ample data or that do not seem significant after careful study of the data.

- Continue to revise the outline until you feel it is a good representation of the data you have collected.

Exercise 9: Data analysis with children

Have children use the chart in Figure 7–2 to help them analyze their data.

Data source	Theme #1:	Theme #2:	Theme #3:	Theme #4: (outliers)
Observations				
Student work samples				
Reflective journal				
Photographs				

Eight

Telling Your Story

o o o

*H*aving made it through the data analysis process, you now face the challenge of putting together the findings of your research. The most important thing to do as you tell this story is to present compelling evidence for your claims and to make a thoughtful, insightful, and clear analysis of it.

You may experience a pleasant surprise when you get involved in the process of writing up the story of what you have learned. If you planned your study carefully and analyzed your data throughout to extract major themes or ideas, you may find that the writing part can be a creative and rewarding experience.

There are many ways to tell your story. You can tell it as a straightforward report, describing what you saw through vignettes and quotations from the data. You can enhance this report with illustrations, photos, work samples, or other summarized data, perhaps displayed in charts or graphs, which show how often and under what contexts you saw certain behaviors or reactions. Another way to tell your story is to weave your themes, backed up by your data, into a narrative written in either the first or third person. Or, you can craft your findings into an account of an event or events from the perspective of different participants. Still other ways to share your findings are to use your evidence to put together a hypothetical "day-in-the-life" of a child or a classroom, or to paint a portrait of a child. Or, you might string together "telling cases" that epitomize your major themes. A metaphor might even emerge that will serve as the organizer for your story.

All along, since you first thought of your research topic, you may have had a sense of the final product. For you, the selection of a writing format and style for your findings may flow from your research questions and the problems you explored in your inquiry. However, if you have not yet considered how to tell the story of your research and if you are not sure what format or style might be a good fit with your research questions, one way to begin to craft the final research product is to look at published qualitative studies or unpublished teacher research that have captured your attention in the past. Reading studies of others' research can help you select a style of writing for your findings that matches with your research topic and questions. In Appendix 1 at the end of the book, we have gathered some references of published teacher research that we think you might find instructive.

Different ways to tell your story

There is no single correct way to write up your research. In the work of the many teacher researchers we know, we have seen numerous and creative ways to report findings. Many teacher inquirers mix two or more ways of writing up findings—some provide student work to illustrate changes over time; some even use photographs to tell what they have learned from their studies.

A report of the themes in the data   *A report of the themes in the data*

Typically teacher researchers share what they have learned in a report format that identifies and explains the themes of their findings. Often, the researcher gives each important theme or pattern that emerged in the data analysis a separate subsection and a subtitle in the write-up. Each theme is introduced by explaining how often this theme came up in the data and under what conditions. A study that is rich with examples from the data of student talk, work samples, and other sources should help its reader imagine the classroom setting.

Here is an example of how to present the themes of your findings in the form of a report. It is excerpted from Natalie's study of how to support students' independent literacy learning in centers. Organized around the themes that she developed through her data analysis, Natalie began with a simple introduction.

> Over the course of the sixty days I researched my kindergarten class, I found several main themes (some the same as my subquestions and other slightly different) emerge from my data.

Natalie then listed her themes, devoting a section to an explanation of each, selecting examples, quotes, and pictures that best represented the recurring patterns that she identified. Here is an excerpt from one section of Natalie's findings about the theme "Children teach themselves and each other through self-discovery, collaboration, and sharing."

I witnessed many conversations and collaborative work during the reader's and writer's workshop center play. Here [referring to a displayed photo] we see a group of students working with their independent reading texts and discussing what they are writing.

Another area where I saw a lot of collaborative planning and discussion was the block area. The children decided what they wanted to build first, and then worked together to accomplish the goal. Oftentimes one suggested standing on a chair or enlisted the help of a taller student to get the job done. The point is that the children came up with creative ways to problem solve and be successful.

On January 27th I witnessed some collaborative discovery when one literacy center group was making flip books and was trying to figure out how to work the ministapler I had bought. One child took charge, manipulated it for a few seconds, and then showed everyone else in the group how to use it.

I frequently saw children helping or coaching each other through the learning process. On February 23rd I saw Aryana looking over Jed's shoulder as he was reading. She was encouraging him and talking about the book. On February 25th I witnessed two boys and one girl writing sentences to go with the paintings they just made. The girl was going from one boy to another, helping them sound out and reminding them to leave spaces. I often saw children reminding each other to write the date on their papers.

I have also witnessed my children take initiative in their learning. In February, Ronald was in the flip books center and he told me that there were no flip books in there he liked and he was going to make his own.

It is clear from the observations that the kindergartners relate to each other in ways that help them create deeper understandings. One way they effectively act on these understandings is through play.

Notice how Natalie continually used examples and references from her data to back up and explain her ideas.

Writing a narrative ◉ Narrative writing is another form you can select to write up your findings. There are many choices of writing styles even within narrative writing. Some researchers write in the first person, telling a story from their own perspective. In the following example, Shenaz presented the findings of her research in a story that detailed the process of her own inquiry. She recounted how she did her study, explaining both the process she went through as well as what she learned, by referencing examples from the data she collected. Here is an excerpt from one part of her story that describes how she learned to manage reading conferences during her Reading and Writing Workshop:

When I started [my study], my goal was to meet with four to five students. This was difficult because conferences last about five minutes. Meeting with four students alone requires my students to be reading for twenty minutes! That is a lot to ask of a first grader in October and November. On November 20, 2003, I noted in my personal journal that it was hard to meet with four or five students. I was meeting with two, sometimes three. It wasn't until December 3rd that I realized that it was acceptable not to be able to meet with so many students individually during reading workshop.

Shenaz continued her narrative by describing how she came to manage writing conferences and what she did with the information about her students that she gained through the conferences, describing each child she studied and how each developed. Samples of students' work, as well as excerpts from students' records and Shenaz' journal were used to illustrate the points that she made. She ended her story with reflections about what she still needed to do to continue to improve both her reading and her writing conferences:

In my personal journal I note on several occasions (11/20, 12/02, 12/11, 1/06, 1/14, and 1/19) that I am not commenting on what my students are doing well or what strategies they are using. I know that this is an important part of the conference. Not only does it make them feel good, but it also gets them thinking and talking about the strategies. If students are aware of the strategies they are using, then they will more likely use them.

An account utilizing the perspective of different participants ○ For teacher researcher Kisha Pressley's findings from her study of how three parents of the children in her kindergarten class supported their children's literacy at home, she composed narratives of the three mothers in which they discussed their personal learning histories and their philosophies of educating their own children. After the narrative section of the findings, Kisha looked across all three of the narratives for commonalities in the mothers' beliefs. Here she discusses one of the themes that she found: How the mothers support their children's emergent literacy by making learning materials available in their homes.

Karen says that Alicia has her own bookshelf with about one hundred books passed on from an older cousin. "Alicia has a lot of books with cassettes to it and she'll play them over and over again." She bought Alicia workbooks and has magnetic letters on the refrigerator. She also informed me that her daughter has a laptop at home. Karen plays monopoly with Alicia because she feels that it will strengthen her weak mathematic skills. She also wants her to learn to count money. "I want her to learn to count better."

Pamela tells me that Carl is in a book club where she orders his CD-ROMs. Carl has a "whole little library of books he reads at home." She believes firmly that he learns from those. He has cassette tapes of storybooks and he also has "interactive books and toys." In addition to this he uses the Internet at his grandmother's house. Although Pamela says she does not know "where he learns much of the stuff," she told me that she bought him a basic curriculum book for pre-K and was able to tell me all the areas of the curriculum it covers.

Rosalind told me that Tameka has her own books stored away in a hutch that she is able to reach. "I belong to a book club and so does Tameka." Tameka has interactive ABC books and other interactive books. She has letter magnets, alphabet blocks, toys, and puzzles. Rosalind says she recently got a new computer and is currently looking for CD-ROMs for Tameka. Rosalind subscribes to *Essence* and *Vibe* magazines. In fact, she tells me that it is not uncommon to find Tameka trying to read the magazines.

A day in the life of a child ◦ Michelle, who conducted a study asking how she could better serve a child (Kareem) with special needs in her mainstream classroom, decided to share her data as "A Day in Kareem's Classroom Life." She looked through the data for examples that were representative of what she saw everyday. For example:

It's 8:15 AM and Kareem enters the classroom with his sister and brother. He says "Good morning" and puts his coat in his cubby and washes his hands. He goes to the Math Center and begins to play with dominoes and explains his understanding of how to play the game to me. He says "When you get this game youb [sic] have, two bive [sic] of dees [sic] you put them right here," (pointing to two sets of five orange circles on the dominoes and then placing them five orange circles to five orange circles) (tape recording, 3/13/03). He continues to explore math using the counting bears. He begins by using his right hand to take out a green bear, a yellow bear, and then a blue bear ...

Using her documented observations as evidence, Michelle continued in the story of her findings to show Kareem's understanding of math concepts and his fine motor skills. After sharing one representative observation, Michelle explained how Kareem generally approached math problems and then discussed his strengths and weaknesses in this area. Michelle's story of Kareem's day provides rich details for the reader and leaves the reader with a strong sense of this child.

A day in the life of a school ⊙ If you decide to use the narrative form of "a-day-in-the-life" to share the findings of your study, it is important that you use great care to choose what data to include and not include. Each example should represent evidence you have seen repeatedly and that effectively characterizes your research subject or events.

Allison presented her findings from her study of multiple intelligences by creating a "day-in-the-life" of the classroom that she studied for almost a year. It is a collage of carefully chosen excerpts from her conversations with students and teachers, photographs of the classroom, and samples of children's work. Her description began with the morning transition from home to school and followed the children throughout the school day to the morning meeting, time spent at reading and writing workshops, music, math, science, dance, art, and the afternoon transition from school to home. Although the activities depicted did not all actually happen during the course of one day, Allison's portrait wove them together hypothetically to demonstrate how the teaching she observed was responsive to the differing strengths, needs, and styles of learning of the diverse learners in the class. Here is an excerpt from her story:

> It is 8:30 AM. The halls of the school are busy with families, teachers, and school personnel getting to where they're going. As I meander through the crowd, toward the K–1 class I am observing, I see a child reaching toward his representation of one hundred things, to show his dad. I hear a mother asking her child where to put his lunch box as the child is taking his two-year-old brother into his classroom. As I enter the classroom I see another two-year-old sibling notice the other and exclaim, "Eli!" as he rushes to hug him. Meanwhile, the students of the class begin their work. Some children go to read the greeting board, which has the morning activity of: "Find a word from a poem that you can read and write it here." The children enthusiastically go about the task, often using another peer or a parent for help or reassurance. Some children are busy signing in on the attendance sheet and putting their name on the attendance board. I notice the classroom teacher take notice of a child having a tough time after separation from her mom. The teacher asks, "Are you OK?" and

the child nods a response. "Are you sure?" the teacher asks
while touching the child.

Other children have moved to observe and draw representa-
tions of the crickets [cricket drawings are provided].

Three children move to the block area and work together
on a structure that was left from the previous day [a photo
of children in the block area is provided].

Other children go to observe the mealy worms [photo is
provided]. "My worm was picking his head up." "Mine isn't
walking." "Mine is doing gymnastics!"

After a verbal cue to finish within five minutes, the teacher
then uses a musical cue to begin the transition to the meeting area. She claps a rhythm pattern and children mimic the
pattern. She then moves to a song countdown as children
put away projects … and move to the rug.

Allison's written descriptions are enriched by a stunning photographic
display and are interspersed with her own commentary that offers an
ongoing analysis of the story:

In this sample of the typical morning rush and transition from
home to school, I am made aware of all the learning that is
occurring. Support for naturalistic, linguistic, spatial, and personal intelligences intermingle as the morning begins. The
naturalistic intelligence is supported by the fact that the classroom is an ongoing science laboratory, evidenced by young-
sters choosing to study the crickets and mealy worms, and
record their observations in drawings as they share with each
other what they see. Support for linguistic intelligence
abounds as children sign in; read the greeting board; work on
the activity; talk with their peers, parents and teacher, etc. …"

Portrait of a child ● For teacher researcher Tabitha Perez's findings about
her study of her experience teaching one of her first grade students how
to read using the Orton–Gillingham approach, she "painted a picture of
John's learning experiences" in her classroom. She did this by first describ-

ing both John's background and her own. She then described John as a learner at the beginning of the year by carefully analyzing work samples. Next, she explained her teaching philosophy and how she used the Orton–Gillingham approach with John. Then, through work samples, she showed how John's reading evolved during the course of the year. She also included how his attitude changed and how his mother's hard work played an important role in the changes in his abilities throughout the year. Tabitha's meticulous collection of work samples and accompanying analysis of John's work document his experiences over a school year in an almost visual way that provide the reader with a clear picture of what happened in her classroom.

In the following example, Tabitha discusses one of her identified themes: John's increasing excitement about reading throughout the school year. She supports this theme with ample evidence and citations from her data. Tabitha begins this section of her findings with a subtitle and an introduction:

> *John's Excitement for Reading*
>
> The biggest change that I have seen from John is his excitement for reading. John's confidence as a reader has soared. This wasn't apparent at the very beginning of the school year. After a short while I noticed him taking books out of his desk more frequently, going over to the library area after he completed his work, and ordering books from the Scholastic Book Club that the class participates in.

Tabitha continues to describe this theme by providing examples from her different data sources (in the following section she cites her research journal). Note how she uses words like "often" and "once" to give the reader a sense of how common these occurrences were.

> Often now, when John has finished his work, he will take a book out of his desk and use his book marker to keep track of the words while he is reading (Journal, p. 1, 5, and 6). When John reads he concentrates deeply. It is almost like he is inside the book. Once John was on the rug reading a book and there were children mumbling around him and he paid them no attention. Even when I sat next to him he just looked up at me and them back down at the book (Journal, p. 7).

Tabitha goes on to cite conversations she had with his mother about John's interest in the public library, and his improvement in standardized test scores. Her examples from multiple data collection sources show the reader how she has triangulated her data—she has seen John's excitement about reading from a variety of perspectives.

Although each of these examples demonstrates how findings can be reported in a different way, the element that they have in common is their constant referencing of evidence to support the assertions made.

Finding a "good fit"

As you approach the write-up of your findings, it is important to select a style of writing that matches with your research topic and questions. For instance, if your study is a "shadow study" in which you followed a child through a day of his or her life (Burnaford, 2001) and the purpose of the study is to see school from the perspective of this child, you may want to write the findings as a narrative from the point of view of the child. On the other hand, if you are studying one teaching method in the context of your classroom, you may want to share some themes from the data that show your classroom's unique community and context, and share charts that demonstrate the regularity of certain behaviors in relation to the methods you are studying. Or, if you are looking at one child's growth during the course of a school year, you may write about the big issues you have identified about his development and show his progression through work samples that you annotate for the reader.

To ensure a "good fit" for your study, you may want to play with the themes you developed as you analyzed your data and try out different styles to see what might make the most sense. As you sit down to write, it is important to think about the potential readers of your study. Who would you like to read the study, and what would you like them to get out of it? How can you make this material accessible? To help you decide how to proceed, it may be helpful to get outside input. Try sharing sample findings written in different styles with a critical friend.

Getting started

Once you have selected a way of writing up your findings, look back over your data analysis notes and choose data you want to use to illustrate what you have learned. You may choose to display your data explicitly or use it to craft your story in creative ways, such as the "day-in-the-life" or "portrait" examples presented earlier. Ely et al. (1999) suggest sharing both representative examples from the data and powerful single examples. For example, you may see a clear pattern in your data of your students demonstrating a certain reaction. You can look through these examples and share one or two quotations or vignettes of these reactions as representative examples. On the other hand, there may be a single moment that surprised you for some reason, that caused you to think about your research project differently, or that made you question your assumptions in some way. These anomalies may be illuminating and should also be shared with the reader.

Describing your choices as a researcher
As you think through your choices in writing your findings, you may want to open an additional document on your computer or paper notebook where you can jot down your thoughts. Your decisions of what to share in your findings should be as systematic as possible. Make sure to include data that are representative. What is not representative should be examined to determine whether it reveals something else important that you want to discuss. You may choose to include it for that reason. Reflect on your choices by asking yourself some of the following questions:

- What examples are you leaving out of the findings and why?

- Why are you choosing to include certain elements of the story of the study and not others?

- Are there areas of the data that seem too messy, inconclusive, or contradictory that you are ignoring?

- What are you going to do about these "messy" pieces of data?

These reflections are important to note so that, when writing up your findings, you can describe these decisions for the readers of your study. In addition, look back at the research journal you have been keeping and include in this section other aspects of the study, such as the conditions of data collection and how your thinking changed throughout the process. As mentioned earlier, being explicit about the choices you have made is an important way to ensure a reliable study. By sharing your perspective and thinking in constructing the findings, you are acknowledging that yours is only one way to tell this research story, that it is not the absolute "Truth." Barone (1995) reminds us that "a story never tells the absolute truth"

(p. 64), and reminds researchers that storytelling, or narrative, is "historically contingent, never impervious to social conditions within a specific culture and time" (p. 64). Remember that the research story you present is influenced by the participants' and your own experiences, words, and beliefs, as well as by various research and social conventions.

Creating a complex picture

Regardless of the style or format of writing that you select for sharing your findings, you want to strive to create a complex picture of the participants (Ely et al., 1999), rather than a simple two-dimensional portrayal. Everything in your study will not fit together neatly. Don't try to force it to do so. Instead, embrace the complexity of your study. It is only when you have to think through seemingly contrary ideas that you can share a more complicated and honest picture with the reader. In creating this complex picture, you will likely want to provide the reader of your study with a careful description of the lives of all the participants in the study—teachers, students, parents and guardians, or others. You can quote from your data to highlight aspects of their lives. When doing this, you may want to reference the data sources in the same way that you cited authors within the text of your literature review (as seen in the previous examples of teacher researchers' work). By doing this, you help to establish your study's reliability. If readers want to reanalyze your study and data, they can use these citations to help them.

Conducting a member check

Just as you did for your data analysis, you can conduct a "member check" of your findings. Doing this offers the potential to provide you with valuable information. A member check for your findings usually entails sharing your working findings with the participants of the study and asking them for their thoughts and feelings about how they are depicted. Many qualitative researchers insist that member checks are necessary to ensure that the voices and perspectives of the participants are represented. "[S]ilence is created when those who are the subjects of research have little or no power in the construction of accounts about them, no access to texts, and no avenues into the corridors of knowledge–production power" (Lincoln, 1993, p. 32).

After sharing the findings with the participants, you may want to include in your final version of the findings how the participants reacted to your draft of the findings. Did anything about their reaction surprise you? Did their analysis give you any insights you had not originally seen?

Valuing your teaching actions as part of the research

Often teacher researchers find that their research has helped the participants of their study with an issue they discovered while conducting it. During the course of the study the teacher researchers, because of what they have learned from their investigation, may have had occasion to call community agencies on a student's behalf, visit a student's home, find resources for families, or tutor children after school—all while wearing their joint teacher/researcher hats. Actions like these are enormously relevant to your teacher research study (they are often examples of the "action" part of action research) and should be included in the findings.

For example, Michelle, who studied her special needs student, Kareem, interviewed his mother as part of the data collection process. During the interviews Michelle learned that Kareem's mother, who Michelle had previously thought was in denial about her son's needs, had a strong interest in her child's education. From that point on, Michelle and Kareem's mother worked together. Michelle included a description of this revelation and of her developing relationship with Kareem's mother in her story of her study. She described sharing with the mother both the readings she did for her study as well as information that she found about a related local service agency that could provide speech services for the child while he was in daycare. Michelle also directed the mother to Internet links related to speech issues in young children, and even a website that had a chat room for caregivers of children with speech delays. In the write-up of her findings, Michelle discussed how she helped Kareem's mother by serving as a person who listened to her concerns. These details enriched Michelle's story as well as demonstrated the impact of her study.

Drawing conclusions and implications from your inquiry

As you come to the end of your research journey, take some time to reflect on what you have learned so that you can formulate some conclusions. Review the big ideas you discovered in your findings and summarize them. Connect them to ideas you have read about from other authors. Think about what these findings mean, not only for you as a teacher, but for other teachers and others in our profession as well. Consider what new questions have been generated by your investigation. And finally, think about the process you went through as you conducted your investigation.

Summarize your findings ⊙ As you review what you have learned to draw your conclusions, think about if you found something new or if your study provided evidence for prior notions that were only intuitive. What do you think about what you learned? What, if any, realizations has your study brought forth—about your teaching, about children, about curriculum, etc? As a result of your study, did you become aware of something you had not noticed before? Have you come to appreciate something you had not valued before?

Connect your understandings to the literature you read ⊙ Think back to the literature you read about your questions. Did you confirm what you read earlier or did your study lead you to disagree? Has conducting your study led you to uncover something new or to see the literature in a different light? Did the context of your classroom or school affect your study's results differently than in other studies you read?

Draw implications for yourself as a teacher ⊙ How has your study changed your thinking and/or your teaching practice? Ask yourself the following questions:

- How have your understandings of your students as learners changed?
- What kind of input have you received from your students that has changed your teaching?
- What new understandings did you gain about your students' caregivers, your colleagues, your administrators, or the school community?
- What did you learn about your teaching methods?
- How might you adapt your teaching in the future based on your findings?
- What have you learned about yourself as a learner and how will this impact your future teaching?

Your study may also lead to implications beyond your own classroom. You may ask yourself additional questions such as the following:

- If your study involved others, did it help them to develop new understandings or to ask new questions? How?
- Did your relationships with administrators change during this process? In what ways?

- How might what you have learned in this study be helpful to others—teachers, administrators, families, your community, the profession at large?

- How can you share what you have learned with your colleagues in your school, district, or the profession?

Questions to study further ◦ Often questions lead to other questions. Consider the following: What questions that you had when you began your study still remain unanswered? What new questions have emerged through the process of investigating? What might you do next to follow up on these questions?

Reflect on your inquiry journey ◦ So much has happened since you began your study. What were some of the best moments you experienced? What problems and challenges did you face? How has the research process impacted you as a learner?

In the following study, Natalie describes what she learned during her study, how she grew from its inception, and what her learning means for her future teaching:

> I set out originally to investigate how I could improve the way I support independent learning through literacy center play. I knew from the start the impact that play has on development (National Association for the Education of Young Children, 1986, 1988, 1989, 1997), but I wanted to concretize my understandings by directly observing my students and simultaneously reflecting on what I was seeing.
>
> I found that during learning center time, my children, while engaged in meaningful literacy activities, made some of the most important discoveries and were approaching many of the milestones on the continuum of child development. Young children need to be actively involved in everything they are learning. Whether it is with manipulatives, with dramatic play and props, with creative art activities, planning what to construct in the blocks, or even just adding their own prior knowledge to an activity, they internalize at an optimal level when they are active. The way for young children to be active is to play.

In my classroom, since I have begun teaching with the balanced literacy approach as a model, I am creating situations in centers, where the children have a space to play, control their own learning, and absorb the information. Kindergarten is about sorting through the massive amount of sensory experiences, emotional stresses, and cognitive strains that are put on a child so young. Play allows a certain amount of freedom from risk and limitations, allowing the children to become more autonomous.

In observing my class of kindergarten students I was able to see how crucial it is for the teacher to be in tune with the needs and interests of the children in front of her. I was able, by taking anecdotal notes, and in turn, reflecting on said notes, to explore exactly what my children kept coming back to and what they really enjoyed. I then proceeded to make curriculum adjustments and differentiated lesson plans to accommodate the varied desires of my students. This approach has afforded me the power to know what each child needs and how to address these needs.

This study has reminded me of the importance of reflecting on my own practice to improve it and to avoid becoming stagnant. The little people who sit in front of me every day are constantly changing, growing, and experiencing through school and other places. It is my job to give them certain tools, especially related to literacy and math, in order for them really to understand their sensory experiences. I think what I have learned is highly significant because I am becoming a more reflective individual who is dedicated to scaffolding young independent learners. I can only hope that my continued reflection, adjustment, and accommodation can benefit the majority of my students.

Putting together a report of your study
When you have finished writing about your findings and your conclusions, you will need to put them together with the rest of the material that you have produced for your study. Review the following outline to guide you.

1. Statement and explanation of your research question

2. Review of literature

3. Research methodology

   a. Description of the participants and setting

   b. Data sources

   c. Data collection methods

   d. Data analysis methods

   e. Permissions/interview and/or survey questions

   f. Time line

4. Findings

5. Conclusions/implications

6. References

7. Appendix (this should include the supporting evidence for your study such as your original notes and other data that you collected)

Each element noted (and explained in each chapter) should be a part of the final version of your research study report. For it, you can follow the template just provided or you can craft a presentation format of your own. Instead of a report, you might want to write an article, make a PowerPoint presentation, create a parent or teacher guide, or set up a website to convey your information. Depending on what format you choose, you will likely need to change what you wrote earlier from the future to the past tense (i.e., sections about research methodology should now describe how you *conducted* rather than *will conduct* your research). If you made changes between what you proposed to do in your study and what you actually did, then include what these changes were and why they happened.

As you review what you are putting together, check to ensure that you have made your findings clear, that you have explained your ideas and backed them up with the evidence that you collected during your investigation, that the ideas from the review of research are connected to the research done for this project, and that you have carefully thought through and explained the implications of what you learned from your study.

A word about writing

How you write your story will make all the difference. It will affect what your readers understand about what you are trying to say as well as affect the impact the findings will have on them. You can increase the power of your ideas by paying attention to the way you develop and organize your ideas, to the language you use, and by making sure that you have mastery over the conventions and mechanics of English, our common language, so that your writing is understandable to all.

Idea development, organization, and language use ◦ Make sure that you have fully explained and elaborated on your ideas. Often writers do not do this enough; what lands on the page is only a portion of the information that is in their heads. Remember, your reader does not have all the context and background information that you have. To bridge the gap between your experience and your readers', you need to provide details and examples as well as clear and focused explanations for all your ideas. These will make your story come alive and be grasped fully by your readers.

Organization is another element of writing that impacts its effectiveness. Try to express your thoughts in a logical progression, moving the reader through the text to showcase and enhance the central ideas of your story. Make sure you have an inviting introduction, thoughtful transitions, and writing that flows smoothly toward a satisfying conclusion.

Choose your words strategically to convey effectively what you want to say. Use your own words instead of language paraphrased or borrowed from books, always citing any authors whose words or ideas you may have used. As you write, listen to the way your words sound and to the cadences of your phrases. Employ the active rather than passive form of verbs. (This makes your writing more direct and understandable.) Make your style appropriate for your purpose and audience.

Keeping these suggestions in mind should help you to unleash and establish your own unique voice.

Mechanics and the conventions of English ◦ Although the most important challenge in any writing is to make it coherent, compelling, and engaging, to show your reader why your topic is important, and to provoke him/her to think about the issues, it is important, too, to pay attention to mechanics and standard writing conventions. This will enhance your writing's readability. Check to make sure that spelling, punctuation, paragraphs, quotation marks, grammar, sentence structure, and other conventions of the English language are used accurately and correctly. Make sure as well that your references and citations follow the appropriate format.

Drafting: Revising and redeeming your ideas ◉ Don't expect to complete the write-up of your study without going through lots of review and revision. All writers need time and lots of drafts to get ideas from the brain onto the paper. "First drafts are for learning what your [work] is about. Revision is working with that knowledge to enlarge and enhance an idea, to reform it" (Malamud, 1975, p. 48). Just as you teach your students to go through "the writing process," you need to go through it as well.

As you try to get your ideas into print, it is not uncommon to feel like you have no idea of what you are doing. Many of the difficulties of writing are really difficulties of clarifying your thinking. What follows are a few suggestions that might help you get your ideas flowing.

Before beginning, try a "free write" (Elbow, 1973). The idea is to write down anything that comes into your head with the rule that you must keep your pen moving continuously. Three pages in a notebook is a good amount. Let the writing take any shape, form, or style and let the content flow in any direction. Don't cross anything out; keep moving forward. This exercise may help you free up your thinking and feel more comfortable putting ideas into words.

Draft an outline, sketch, or "visualization" of the ideas you want to put together in your findings. Refer to these while you are writing to help you stay focused on your intentions.

Once you have gotten started with your writing, you may feel so close to it that you can't see it properly anymore. Try reading through it aloud and jotting down words in the margins that describe what each paragraph is about. After you have finished with this process, review your notes to see if your ideas are progressing or if you are repeating what you already said before.

Once you have completed a draft, utilize peer review—first for content and later for editing details. Ask someone not familiar with your topic to read what you have written to ascertain if the content is understandable. Often we are so familiar with our subject matter that we leave out or gloss over important information. Because this information is "in our heads," we sometimes assume that we have explained it when we have not. Your reader should not have to "second guess" what you have written. Ask your reader to point out the parts that need further explication or that are not expressed clearly (Darling, 2003).

During the early stages of revision, focus on content issues. Concentrate on coherence and organization. Do not obsess about grammatical details. Rearrange or delete sentences, paragraphs, or sections until you feel that your ideas are well communicated. Then review your writing for grammar, punctuation, and other writing conventions. When you are done, ask a friend to review it.

Sharing the final project

When you have completed putting together your final report or story of your study, look for venues to share what you have learned. By "going public" with your work, you help to reveal the dilemmas so many teachers experience in their isolated classrooms (Sanford, 2004).

There are many ways to share your work. You could begin by verbally sharing your learning. You could try getting together in your own "backyard" with other teachers in your grade level or in your school. You could also make a presentation or lead a workshop with other educators in your district or region. Teacher researcher Teresa Roman did both of these kinds of presentations after completing her study of how to support English language learners. She led workshops with the teachers in her school and her district where she shared the strategies and tools she acquired through her study.

If you feel braver, you might even consider writing a proposal to present at a professional conference. Both local and national professional organizations generally hold annual meetings at which members present to each other. Look up the dates on their websites for instructions about how to apply. Be aware that proposal deadlines usually are due many months in advance of the conference. Neurys Bonilla, a Spanish/English-speaking dual-language teacher who did research on the benefits of a multiage classroom, wrote a proposal to present at a professional conference with her colleagues in a teacher research group that she joined after completing her first study. They put together a symposium on classroom-based inquiry that they presented at the University of Pennsylvania's annual Forum on Urban Ethnography.

If you are pleased with your writing and want to share it, there are several ways to do it. You might want to create your own website and post your story for all to see. Or you might want to submit your writing to a journal. Increasingly, journals (both on-line and traditional paper versions) are seeking articles that give voice to teachers' perspectives and concerns. You can find out which ones are interested in teacher research by conducting an Internet search. At each journal's website you should look for its mission statement, call for papers, and/or author guidelines. Review these carefully so that you can have a sense of how to shape your article to increase the likelihood of its being accepted for publication.

If you want to use your writing skills a little bit closer to home, think about writing a newsletter, brochure, or guide that you can use to share information from your study with the families, teachers, and/or administrators in your school or district. This is what teacher researcher Patricia Edwards did after completing her study of how to increase parent involvement. She wrote a report about what she learned and she submitted it to the director of her daycare center. The director found it so informative that she and Patricia turned it into a guide for the teachers in their school.

Kisha did something similar after completing her study of mothers who successfully support their children's literacy development. From her study she identified things that parents can do to support their children's learning. Then she created a guide for parents that was shared with each family in the school community. This guide was particularly helpful to them because it was informed by the experiences of peers from their own community. Kisha explains:

> By using practices in my guide that I learned from parents who share the same culture and context as the other parents in my school, I hope to be increasing the likelihood that others will try some of the suggestions. If I can tell them that these are some of the techniques other single, working parents with "x" number of children have used to produce successful literacy, then they, hopefully, will feel confident that they can achieve the same results with their children.

There are still other ways to share what you learned from your investigation. You might use it to transform not only your own practice but to ignite change in your school and community. This is what colleagues Mercedes Orozco, a native of Mexico, and Betty Kouassi, a native of Harlem, where they both work, did together in their school after they each completed an inquiry about their practice. They were so inspired by the experience that they teamed up to co-teach. Together they worked on transforming their classrooms into communities of inquiry. They reached out to utilize the resources of their community, to connect to the families of the children in their classes, and to lead change initiatives with their colleagues, first in their school and later in their district. In addition, they sought National Board for Professional Teaching Standards certification and presented their change initiatives at national conferences. Mercedes credits the research experience as the inspiration for these changes:

> We gained confidence to do this as a result of our research. From it we learned how to choose what we wanted to study and how to think and produce. We learned that research is a never-ending endeavor; that we have to reflect continually on our practices and rethink constantly the understandings of our discipline.

Helping children put together their findings, conclusions, and presentations from inquiry projects

As the investigation and analysis part of children's inquiries draws to a close, it is important to engage them in some kind of culminating project to help them consolidate and reflect on their learning. A culminating project for an inquiry can take different forms, depending on whether the inquiry was conducted by an individual or a group. It will also vary according to the age and skill level of the students.

Individual studies

Much of what has been discussed about your own process for putting together the findings from a study can be applied to how you can help children report their individual investigations. Although a lot of this process involves writing, we do not focus on writing here because there are many excellent books that offer guidance about how to do nonfiction writing with children (see Appendix 5). These are worth consulting to help you hone your skills and get new ideas. Here, however, we offer for your consideration some activities and ideas about how to support children through the process of presenting the learning that they have acquired through their inquiries.

The starting point for writing a report is the data the children collected and analyzed (see Chapter 7). They can begin by looking at their analysis charts and jotting down what they believe are the main themes of findings in their studies. They should be able to explain how these findings relate to the research question and they should be able to elaborate with details, examples, and/or illustrations. Figure 8–1 offers an example of a worksheet that students can use to help them organize their findings.

Figure 8–1. Developing Your Research Findings

What is your research question?

Finding #1:

    Explain this finding with details and/or examples.

    How does this finding relate to your research question?

    Discuss what you think about what you found out. Is it different from what you thought might be the answer? Does this finding raise new questions for you?

Finding #2:

    Explain this finding with details and/or examples.

    How does this finding relate to your research question?

    Discuss what you think about what you found out. Is it different from what you thought might be the answer? Does this finding raise new questions for you?

Finding #3:

    Explain this finding with details and/or examples.

    How does this finding relate to your research question?

    Discuss what you think about what you found out. Is it different from what you thought might be the answer? Does this finding raise new questions for you?

After completing these worksheets, children can share them with each other in pairs or in groups and respond to their classmates' working findings. They can be asked to answer questions such as the ones in Figure 8–2.

The children can respond to these questions in written or discussion forms, depending on their age and the development of their skills. The feedback from these forms can then be given back to each child to use as a resource when writing.

When each student researcher believes that he or she has three to five strong findings, he or she is ready to beginning writing about them. The written findings should address the questions listed earlier; be backed up with details, examples, and explanations (including pictures and drawings if the children choose); and include a conclusion. The conclusions section should summarize the findings and describe implications and any looming questions. Figure 8–3 presents some questions you might ask the children to answer as they prepare to write their conclusions.

Figure 8–2. Peer Response to Working Findings

Does each finding and how it relates to the research question make sense?

Are there examples to explain each finding?

Are the examples clear? Do they offer details and descriptions?

What would you like to know more about?

What questions do you have about the study?

Figure 8–3. Questions to Answer as You Write Your Conclusions

What did you learn?

How does what you learned from your study fit together with what you knew about this topic before?

What do you think about what you learned?

What would you like to find out about this topic or a related topic in the future?

After the children have gone through these processes, they should be ready to put together a completed report. Here is a suggested format to use:

List of questions

An introduction

The written findings (including the children's pictures, drawings, photos, or other evidence)

A conclusion

References

As the children write, they may need assistance with such issues as how to put information from books into their own words, how to organize ideas, how to eliminate repetitive thoughts, how to elaborate ideas, and how to use varied and interesting language. You may want to hold mini lessons about these skills to assist them along the way.

Just as you did with your own inquiry, the children should continually review their work, first to revise and reorganize the content to ensure that it is clear and understandable, then to edit for mechanics and the details of grammar. The writing process can include individual and peer editing, as well as conferencing with you, the teacher.

In addition to writing reports, you may want to have children simultaneously work on projects that demonstrate an aspect of what they are learning. For these, a range of modalities can be used—art, music, drama, and other types of presentations. For example, a study of bridges might be accompanied by a suspension bridge built out of tongue depressors and cord, a study of the blues guitarist B. B. King could feature a music mix of the artist's work, a study of gymnastics might incorporate a gymnastic demonstration, a study of the sun could include a model of the solar system (Falk & Margolin, 2005).

Completed reports and projects can be put on display in the classroom. A presentation of the written report, accompanied by the project, can be a culminating event of the process. Presentations can be followed by class discussions. Here are some guidelines that one class developed to help them listen to each other carefully, process what they heard, and ask useful questions of each other during class discussions (Falk & Margolin, 2005):

Does the question make sense?

Has somebody else already asked this question?

Why are you asking this question?

Pay attention to what has been said.

Think about what it is you want to ask.

Postpresentation conversations have the potential to reveal what the children understand, the connections they are making, or any misunderstandings they may have. For example, in a fourth grade class discussion after a presentation about Rosa Parks, some of the children were confused about the chronology between slavery and the civil rights movement, a common phenomenon among young children. Only by hearing their questions and comments at a class meeting could their teacher know that she needed to use a time line to explain the history of these events (Falk & Margolin, 2005).

Presentations and discussions about individuals' projects can provide the whole class with important information, inspire deep thinking, as well as give them an opportunity to express their feelings and points of view.

Group studies

Culminating experiences of group studies help the whole group to consolidate the learning that takes place in a study. There are numerous kinds of culminating experiences. One is for the class to produce a book that recounts each stage of the group's investigation. The book could include photos, drawings, or other visuals that are annotated and explained by the children's writing or the teacher's writing of children's dictated responses (if the children are very young). The book might even include write-ups of related inquiries conducted by individuals within the context of the group investigation.

Other possibilities for culminating experiences include presentations; constructions such as maps, blueprints, or block building; displays of experiments or art work; or dance, drama, spoken word, or musical performances. Some teachers we know conclude their class' studies with Writers' Celebrations to which they invite their students' families as well as other teachers and students in the school. The visitors read the presenting class' writings and record their responses, impressions, or questions in guest books that are placed around the room. Other teachers we know organize museums in their class at the end of each study. They set up exhibits of the work they have completed for their study and invite different classes and the families of the children to the class to view it. Visitors go around the room to the different displays and listen to a student docent explain what was done and what was learned. Sometimes these events include multimedia presentations, like a puppet show or a play or some other kind of performance.

Generally, culminating experiences for inquiries offer the possibility for students to use a range of modalities to express their learning so that children's different learning styles and strengths can be supported and showcased. The next chapter provides some detailed images of how different classrooms conduct inquiries, put them together, and share them with others.

Exercise 1: Review guide for writing up research findings

Ideas and Content

- Main points are clear and focused with anecdotes.
- Details are provided to support the main ideas.

Analysis

- Evidence for claims is compelling.
- Analysis is thoughtful, insightful, and clear.

Conclusion/Implications

- Central findings are summarized.
- The reader is shown why the topic is important, and is provoked to think about the issues and problems in the study.
- The significance and implications of these findings for the researcher and for teaching in general are discussed.

Organization

- Thoughts are expressed in a logical progression, moving the reader through the text to showcase and enhance the central ideas of the story.
- There is an inviting introduction, thoughtful transitions, and writing that flows smoothly toward a satisfying conclusion.

Language use

- Words are chosen strategically to convey effectively what you want to say.
- Your own words are used instead of language paraphrased or borrowed from others.
- Words or ideas from other authors are cited.
- Writing has a sense of your own unique voice.

Mechanics and the conventions of English

- Spelling, punctuation, paragraphs, quotation marks, grammar, sentence structure, and other conventions of the English language are used accurately and correctly.
- References and citations follow the appropriate format.

Nine

Launching Inquiries from Children's Questions

○ ○ ○

here are many ways to do research with children. Here we offer a look at three different types of inquiries conducted in elementary classrooms. First we very briefly present the process of a research cycle built on children's individual explorations of their own personal questions. Next we describe a study that grew out of an occurrence in a second grade classroom. And lastly, we tell the story of how one class used "work time" to nurture children's individual and group studies through open-ended activities that emanated from the interests and strengths of each learner.

Inquiry Type #1: Individual explorations of personal questions

One way to conduct research with children is to build a curriculum in which children pursue their individual questions in a manner similar to the one for teachers that we have described in this book. The process proceeds something like this: Invite children to brainstorm topics of interest, select an issue to pursue, frame a question and a set of related questions around it, review what other people know about that question, conduct an investigation through a variety of resources and experiences, write about what they have discovered, and present their findings and conclusions in a variety of ways (Falk & Margolin, 2005). This process, influenced by the "I Search" first articulated by Ken Macrorie (1988), can be adapted to the skills and needs of students of varying ages. Suggestions for how to facilitate this process with children have been presented throughout the chapters of this book.

Inquiry types #2 and #3: Individual investigations within the context of group studies

Now we offer some descriptions of other related ways to use children's questions and interests as the starting point of a curriculum. The first account is of a whole-class study in Sue MacMurdy's second grade classroom that demonstrates how curriculum grew out of children's interests about something that happened during the school day. The other story describes how children's individual inquiries can be nurtured through open-ended activities that emanate from the interests and strengths of each learner. It depicts some of the individual and group investigations that grew out of the "work time" in Susan Gordon's fourth grade class, a time set aside during the day when children chose their own activities and actively investigated them in a variety of ways.

The Undersea Study: A whole-class investigation

Sue MacMurdy's second grade class in a small elementary school in the northwest Bronx conducted numerous extended studies during the course of the school year—of human families and homes, of animal homes, of folk tales, of how bridges work, of how plants grow from seeds. Her classroom, made up of children from diverse backgrounds, was furnished with tables and chairs arranged in centers separated by clearly labeled shelves packed with teacher-made, student-made, and commercially made materials for literacy, art, math, and science. Jars of water-brewing experiments, batteries and bulbs, a scale, trays of germinating seeds and plants, as well as aquarium tanks (one with a turtle, the other with fish) occupied the window sills. A rug, delineating a meeting area, was also the center of the classroom library, placed between a book display case and several book shelves containing a wide range of children's fiction, content area books, and reference materials, some arranged by difficulty level, some organized by categories of interest. The walls were filled with children's drawings, writings from their various studies, as well as three-dimensional models, charts, graphs, maps, and posters.

The Undersea Study grew out of several children's intense interest in fish, which was sparked when, earlier in the year, a parent had given the class a water turtle. Live goldfish were a part of the turtle's diet. When the children fed the fish to the turtle, much to everyone's horror and delight, the turtle gobbled them alive within moments. This triggered a flurry of writings and drawings recreating the gory event. It also ignited a curiosity for the study of fish and other undersea phenomena. Sue explains:

> The children's interest in this subject became quite passionate. They pressured me relentlessly to set up an aquarium. While resisting their efforts initially, feeling that I did not know enough to do it properly and worrying that the fish would all end up dead, I eventually relented and took a leap: I consulted with a class member and his parent who had an aquarium, researched the subject with children's books and magazines, and then involved the children in the entire process of planning for, purchasing the equipment, and setting up the tank.

For this study, Sue also involved students in other activities meant to expose them to a variety of related knowledge areas and to connect their interests to broader contexts. Besides several trips to the neighborhood pet shop to purchase fish and related equipment, they visited local sites such as the City Island Undersea Institute, the Museum of Natural History aquatic dioramas, and an exhibit of Alexander Calder's fish mobiles at a nearby museum. They engaged in experiments and activities revealing information about the properties of water, spent hours observing and recording what took place in their own aquarium tanks, perused countless books and magazines about underwater life, and had numerous discussions about the information they were accumulating, the understandings they were developing.

Often Sue would weave the required skills and content of the state standards into the experiences connected to the Undersea Study. She used the district's mandated literacy blocks for readings related to the children's inquiries. She used mini lessons, for individuals or groups, to work on skills as the need arose. (When it was not possible to teach all required content in this way, other group inquiries were designed to make sure that the state standards were being addressed. Within these studies she tried to provide opportunities for individuals to investigate their own areas of interest.)

The culmination of their study was an "Ocean Museum." The children invited each class in the school, as well as their families, to visit their classroom to see exhibits they set up about their study. During this time, the children explained their projects and experiments, and displayed their writings, drawings, and dioramas. There were four different "hands-on" water experiments as well as activities for the visitors, such as making a stuffed fish mobile, all developed by the children in response to queries that arose during their study. Experiment 1 featured different bowls of water that demonstrated the different temperature zones in the ocean. Experiment 2, utilizing empty milk cartons in a water tank, was designed to help participants understand the increasing strength of water as the ocean levels deepen. Experiment 3 demonstrated how to use an instrument that measured water pressure and Experiment 4, utilizing a tuning fork and a tub of water, showed how sound waves travel through the water.

At the Ocean Museum the children also presented a puppet show—"Life Under the Sea." They wrote, designed, produced, and enacted the puppet show themselves. Each class member made a puppet depicting a creature or element of the ocean and then wrote something about their character. Sue wove all the stories together to make the puppet show's script.

At the study's end, the class put together a book of photos and writings that documented the progression of their learning. The book was compiled by asking each child to select a photo from among those taken during the study and at the Ocean Museum, and to write captions explaining the picture. When these were completed, the class got together to reminisce, analyze, and reflect on the process of their work. They commented on each other's writings, offering additional information and making suggestions for the final version of the book. This record of their curriculum's development was placed in the library beside other student/teacher-made books of earlier classroom studies. There it stayed for the children to review as a testament to their collective inquiry.

Work time: Children actively inquire about their own interests

An inquiry curriculum for children can also be built on their individual investigations. These can be conducted individually and shared with the class or used by the whole class as the catalyst for a group study. Susan Gordon's fourth grade class engaged in individual investigations during a time during the day called "work time."

"Work time" in Susan's class took place for about forty-five minutes, three times a week. It was devoted to children's pursuit of their own interests. Utilizing rich resources provided in the classroom, during work time the children chose what they wanted to work on, found a place to do it, and then proceeded to get intensely involved. If you were to walk into this classroom during "work time," you might see lots of things going on at the same time. Some children might be engaged in a book discussion.

Others, alone or in groups, might be working at the computer, reading, working on math or science problems, or actively engaged with materials or experiments. You might find children moving freely about the room, chatting together casually, taking trips down the hall to the library resource room in search of an answer to a question, or returning from mentoring a child in a younger class.

Grounded in Susan's conviction that learning happens best when it is active, social, and based on learners' interests, work time focused on many different kinds of learning, not only the reading/writing modality so emphasized in many schools. Susan explained:

> The curriculum in my class is built on the interests of the kids; the ways in which they approach the world. I bring materials into the classroom that reflect the world, the real stuff of real life. I allow the children to choose what materials they want to work with. I observe and keep careful note of their choices and their ways of approaching things. I spend time thinking and reflecting about their choices and then bring in more materials and suggestions that will extend the children's ideas and offer future directions for their work. Work time in my classroom is set up as a workshop. I believe that everybody has good ideas and that everybody can pursue those ideas. My goal is to provide students with opportunities to use their imaginations and then see what inquiries can evolve from them.

For students who were builders and artists, Susan brought in books about art for them to look at and read. The work of sculptors like Michelangelo and Rodin were made available to Manuel, for example, when sculpting with clay was his passion. For Hugh, Eric, Jose, and Joseph—whose mechanical and artistic inclinations were toward putting things together—Susan brought in recycled junk materials as well as foam board, miniature wheels, axles, and other building materials for them to build with. They used these together to design a cardboard car. For Zenobia and Rene, who continually wrote about, read about, and talked about their families and homes, Susan made materials available for them to build dollhouses. She brought in cardboard boxes, small items to be converted into furniture, reference books filled with construction suggestions, and even wires, batteries, and bulbs so that electricity (a topic of exploration earlier in the school year) could be put into the houses.

Working in this manner, Susan connected the children's interests and ways of learning to the skills and content knowledge required for their grade. She connected their building, drawing, and other kinds of projects to literacy through reading and writing activities; to mathematics through the exploration of topics like measurement and scale; to science through studies in electricity, chemistry, and aerodynamics; to history and social studies through discussions and related trips.

Teaching strategies that support children's individual inquiries ◉ In Susan's classroom, the children's investigations were supported by Susan's careful observation and documentation of what children did, how they approached their work, and what strategies they utilized when doing it. Susan kept ongoing records of individual students as well as a record of the discussions of the whole class. She collected samples of children's work in portfolios. Documenting work in this way allowed her to see the deep themes of learning of her students and to tap into how they integrated their developing understandings. It also enabled her to see the children's strengths rather than focus on their deficits. In one of her reflections in a journal she kept, Susan noted how *"the children are beginning to emerge."*

In addition to picking up on the interests of the students through observations and by bringing in resources to support them, Susan helped children to construct their understandings by reflecting their knowledge back to them during all-class sharing meetings, held after each work time. At these meetings the children would present their work to their classmates or share what they observed, learned, or developed questions about during their work time investigations. Then they would offer each other observations, comments, questions, or suggestions.

Susan charted these questions, observations, and comments for all the children to see. *"I would scribe these ideas because otherwise they would get lost,"* said Susan. Sometimes she would even type them up and distribute them at the next day's meeting. In this way Susan served as keeper of the class' questions and comments. She reflected questions and answers back to the children, picked up the pieces of their learning (kind of like what a good parent does), reminded them about what they already knew, and helped them to connect their ideas to the big ideas of the world. She did this because she understood that children often do not realize what they actually know until it is pointed out to them. She also knew that seeing their work in the context of others' would additionally help them make sense of what they were doing.

The design of the classroom environment was also a key element that supported active inquiry in Susan's classroom. A large work table occupied almost half the room, surrounded by shelves against the walls that housed books, maps, materials for writing and mathematics, supplies for art and cooking, science equipment, and animals such as snakes, hamsters, fish, and a turtle. A water table occupied the narrow hallway leading to the room. A worn blue carpet defined the other half of the room—the meeting area—which was surrounded with books, a computer, maps, charts, and other print materials developed in class studies. Samples of children's artwork and writing were displayed on the walls around the room. Every space in the classroom was utilized for the children's active learning.

Sometimes studies in Susan's classrooms remained as individual or small-group investigations. Other times, because of the interest a topic generated, an individual inquiry turned into a whole-group investigation.

The Flight Curriculum ○ The Flight Curriculum grew out of a trip that Susan's class took to *The Intrepid*, a navy aircraft carrier converted into a museum that is situated on a pier off New York City's Hudson River. After the trip, many students began building planes out of junk materials during work time. They based their constructions on information that the trip provided as well as on research from real books. They built the *Universal*, the *Stealth Bomber*, the *Intruder*, a glider, and helicopters. These creations were shared at class meetings. Through exposure to them, the class talked about history, about design, and about the science and future of flight. Questions arose.

For example, when Hank shared what he was learning about how the design of planes had changed over time, someone asked him, "Why did some of the early two-seater planes have the pilot sit in a back seat?" To answer this question he revisited his history references to fill in the details that he did not know. Or when Akeem shared what he was learning about aerodynamics from the paper air vehicles that he was making, he was asked, "How does a helicopter go forward?" This question led him to experiment more with making paper helicopters to find an answer.

Susan used these questions and interests to introduce books about paper airplanes, which inspired several students to spend many subsequent work time hours creating them. Further questions arising from this work had to do with aerodynamics: What's the best paper? What's the best design? How does a helicopter go forward?

Susan extended the work for some of the children by asking them to make blueprints and maps of their constructions. Presentations of these projects at class meetings led to more questions: How is a helicopter made? How is a medical helicopter different from a regular helicopter? These questions in turn led to discussions of a more philosophical nature: What does "regular" mean?

All the while, Susan scribed notes of these discussions, recording the information as well as philosophical and factual questions. An example is *Our Learnings About Airplanes, Helicopters, and How They Fly*:

1. The way the blades on a fan are positioned affects airflow.

2. The little fan goes faster; it pushes faster.

3. The small fan is lighter.

4. Air makes things float.

5. When you twist the propellers, it flies better.

6. Rudder and tail change the plane's direction.

7. The rudder catches the wind and pulls the plane back.

8. The propeller sucks in the air and gives it more of a thrust.

9. If it flies or if it crashes, it's like floating and sinking. It depends on the design and the material it's made of.

10. 1919—the first trans-Atlantic flight by Alcock and Brown

11. The Cessna plane is a sports plane.

12. The *Intruder* plane was a bomber plane used in Vietnam.

13. We should recycle planes.

14. The early planes were made of canvas, bamboo, and wood.

15. They were biplanes and triplanes.

16. They had no propeller.

17. The *Stealth Bomber* moves by thrust.

18. The *Universal* plane was the first to use radar. It was made in WWII.

19. A future transporter plane will be solar powered with an electric battery storage system.

20. Propellers on top of helicopters are called rotors. They turn and pull the helicopter up.

21. It goes up like a tornado.

22. The helicopter flies at an angle to make it go forward.

23. The forces from the front and back equalize it.

The class regularly reviewed these charts. Each time they discussed what they needed to talk about more, what additional information they needed to continue their study, and what they needed to do to go forward in pursuit of their questions. They learned to distinguish what was true from what was false and they learned to differentiate between opinions and facts. Here Susan reflects on these discussions:

> These discussions were the most exciting part of our day. I never knew where a conversation was going to take us. I never knew where a day would end and what we were all going to get out of it. The work seemed literally to generate itself.

The Bubble Study: Moving from the concrete to the abstract ◦ Work time investigations usually began with "hands-on" explorations. Only after this kind of concrete learning would the class consult books or other outside information. The class' Bubble Study is an example of how this process worked. It began with opportunities during work time for children to explore bubbles at the water table, observe and document what they were doing, and raise questions about the strength, size, structure, and colors of bubbles. After each work time the class met to share developing observations and to raise new questions. The questions, which were recorded on large chart paper that hung on the walls in the meeting area, helped to shape plans for the next few days' work.

By following the progression of the children's ideas, Susan gradually introduced other materials and ideas. For example, the class examined solutions, layers in solutions, baking chemistry, mystery powders, salt, and heat. After an extended period of time experimenting with bubbles, discussing findings, generating and answering questions, the class put together *The Bubble Book*. They put it together by first going through the charts that had recorded all their observations and questions. Next, they discussed what they had discovered and decided what information was true and what was false. Only after they completed this process did they consult all the books about bubbles that they could find in the library. To their surprise and delight, the class found out that, through their own experimentation, they had already discovered most of the known facts about bubbles that were in the published books. They then prepared their own book and published it on the computer, complete with illustrations. Susan called this process *reverse learning*.

Susan had a great time while the class was conducting these studies. She was a learner right alongside the students, frequently bringing her own curiosity and questions to the children's work. She did not hesitate to put out her own ideas for the children to come up against or to argue with: "Gee, I wonder if . . ." or "I don't think that's right." Yet she also remained cautious about not letting her ideas dominate others'. She consciously tried to use her questions to extend and bring enthusiasm to the investigations. Susan's reflection on this phenomenon was as follows:

> I was a learner just like the kids. I didn't have all the
> answers. In fact, when a study of a particular topic took
> hold in the room, the way I found out about it was to read
> as much as I could find in all the "kid books," the Internet,
> and the encyclopedia. If the kids needed to go deeper in
> pursuit of their questions, they would need to call an
> expert or go to a museum.

The children, too, enjoyed learning in this way. Their comments reveal their feelings:

> Instead of reading about something, you do it and because you
> want to learn about something, you try hard and learn more.

> When you are interested in something you don't learn about
> that subject because someone tells you the answers; you
> study it and learn it in your own way.

> In most schools you get told what to do but never get your
> questions answered. In this class your questions are
> answered so you feel better about asking them.

Through this way of working, each child was able to find an area in which he or she excelled and to become valued by the others as an "expert" in that area. This valuing of their strengths helped the children to appreciate each other. The inner and outer circle of academic success (a class divided into "smart" and "not-so-smart" kids), prevalent in so many school settings, broke its hold in this classroom. The children explained it in this way:

> We learn not only from ourselves, but from other people's ideas and find information from each other.

> This class brings out your talents.

How teachers can support children's questions

Supporting children to inquire and to investigate challenges us teachers to redefine our roles and to shift our focus away from what children *do not* know and what they *cannot* do, to what they *do* know and what they *can* do.

Another challenge that teaching to encourage questioning involves is to shift the role of the teacher from a giver of information and a provider of answers to an observer of children and a facilitator of the learning environment. Teaching to support children's pursuit of questions calls on us to listen to children's voices closely, to value and respond to their concerns, and to ask questions of them that increase their understandings, call attention to the contexts in which other questions arise, and suggest opportunities for more observation and more thoughts (Osborne & Freyberg, 1985):

> Can you find a way ...?

> Have you seen anything new?

> Why do you think?

> What do you think happens if?

> How might we find out?

It also demands that we pose questions to ourselves about how best to facilitate a study's development:

> How do I extend?

> When do I extend?

> When do I jump in and when do I stay out?

Elements of a curriculum built around questions

The stories from Sue and Susan's classrooms share characteristics that help to clarify how to support children's inquiries.

The studies were born out of the interests and the initiatives of the students. The teachers took children seriously and showed an appreciation for their real questions. Sue credits the children's intense involvement in their work to this:

> The investment of the children was much greater when they had the opportunity to make their own choices. The secret I have learned from this is that children have their own work. If we allow them the opportunity, they will do it, and learn from it, and retain it far better than if we were to give it to them.

Susan also found this to be true:

> Before I changed the way I worked, the kids were assigned projects. They would finish them and then come to me and say, "All right, what do I have to do next?" Now I don't get that anymore because the kids have their own work. They know what they want to do and they do it. They are much more autonomous.

For each study, the teachers found ways to utilize the diverse learning styles and strengths of the particular children involved. Children were encouraged to explore their thinking and solve problems through a wide range of materials and in a wide range of ways—through reading and writing, for example, as well as through talking, building, or art. Being allowed to work at their own pace and difficulty level as well as to express their own unique ways of seeing the world gave children confidence as learners and thinkers, most dramatically for those who were insecure about their abilities. Some tried things at which they had not previously been successful or were reluctant to do in other contexts. Discipline problems also seemed to fade away. As children pursued their interests, the culture of the classroom seemed to change. The children became more focused and confident, and camaraderie grew.

Diversity was supported and respected in these classrooms in other ways too. No one "right" way to do things was held up; but, rather, there was an open-ended, flexible appreciation for different ways of approaching and thinking about problems and issues. In class meetings, the teachers welcomed different strategies or solutions to problems. They recognized that one person's strategy might open up an understanding for another and that the children's process of explaining their ideas to others helped them to articulate and solidify their thinking. Children learned to ask each other questions and rely on each other to work things through. As they shared information and helped each other find resources and learn new skills, a sense of community evolved through their work.

Each of the studies described here took place over relatively long stretches of time—several weeks or more. There were no pacing calendars for these investigations. Meaning was not sacrificed for speed and efficiency. Understanding, thinking things out deeply, having continuity of thought were what was valued. Susan explains:

> These things happened over really long periods of time. Kids would often leave this work and go back to it at a later time. I left lots of room for them to explore and to finish things. I never let something go because we had already studied it. Kids seemed to have a natural desire to revisit old ideas. This was another secret that I learned—that things don't ever finish.

Questions often led to bigger issues that carried across different units of study in the investigations in both Sue's and Susan's classes. The learning that took place in these classrooms was not artificially divided into distinct fields or subject matters. It was connected to real life, intertwined and interconnected, containing possibilities for multiple interpretations and multiple entry points. The teachers helped their students use ideas and the thinking that evolved out of this work to connect to big ideas. In this way, the studies helped children deepen their understandings and expand their thinking.

Working in this way suggests a new notion of the term *integrated curriculum.* It is a notion that reconceptualizes curriculum as an opportunity for awakening and pursuing questions, an opportunity for each learner to discover and integrate knowledge in his or her own way. This integration of learning is an act of the learner, not a presentation of the teacher. This is very different from what happens with traditional curricula where everyone is given the same information to process in the same way; where the sense making and connections have already been done by the writers of the curriculum before being given to the students to "learn." In contrast, the inquiry research approach described here challenges students to construct and synthesize their own understandings as an integral part of doing the curriculum.

Challenges for teachers

It is hard to follow learners' interests and questions in today's high-stakes testing environment. To meet mandates and prepare for tests, some teachers simply follow prescribed curricula. But Sue and Susan demonstrated that there are other ways to do this. They managed the tension between what they believed was best for children's learning and the requirements of their district and state by prepping for tests minimally but efficiently, and incorporating required skills and knowledge into the "lessons" they conducted for their research curricula. When such connections could not be made, they balanced individual studies with whole-group studies on themes that explicitly addressed the standards. Even within the prescribed content of the group studies, however, they always tried to offer choices for individual children, persisting in providing relevant opportunities for students to learn about the world in authentic ways.

Another challenge for these teachers was time. When they first began launching sustained investigations in their classrooms, they felt overwhelmed by the amount of time needed to individualize curriculum and to assess the work for each child in their large classes. As they gained more experience, however, the work became easier. They realized that finding the time and energy to think about students, to attend to individuals while building community, to gather and prepare the resources needed for their learning, to record students' ongoing growth and development, and to engage in their own professional development is the challenge as well as the joy of teaching.

Curiosity
The Secret to Wisdom

○ ○ ○

...The wise woman listened, and laughed. "My dear child, you have found the secret." Jenny was puzzled. "How can I have found it?"

"Because, you see, the secret to wisdom is to be curious—to take the time to look closely, to use all your senses to see and touch and taste and smell and hear. To keep on wandering and wondering."

"Wandering and wondering," Jenny repeated softly.

"And if you don't find all the answers, you will surely find more to marvel at in this curving, curling world that spins around and around amid the stars."

—Merriam (1991)

Like Jenny, in the story cited here, we and other teachers who have pursued questions along with our students have discovered our curiosity, wandering and wondering our way toward new wisdom, learning, and growth. Many of us have been exposed to new knowledge, issues, teaching methods, and strategies. Others of us have deepened our understandings or made meaning out of knowledge that we thought we already knew. Some of us have found affirmation for previously intuitive ideas and practices or changed our attitudes toward our work.

Many of us have come to recognize what a powerful motivator to learning interest can be. We have been transformed into more eager, capable, and confident learners, becoming reflective about our practice, developing a disposition for life-long learning, seeing ourselves as professional educators, and gaining a new sense of possibility about our work.

Teacher research: Transformative possibilities

Here are some examples of changes that have happened to some of the teachers we know as a result of their teacher research experiences.

New learnings

Conducting research has helped teachers we know to consolidate new knowledge, learn about new issues, and develop new teaching methods and strategies. Ignacia's study of second-language acquisition gave her the opportunity to familiarize herself with the research of this field and to test it out in her classroom. In her close-up observation of three children, she watched and learned how language acquisition theories played out. Likewise, Yolanda Serrano's study of kindergartners who had not previously attended school bolstered her knowledge of developmental and cultural differences. Through her study she learned that there are variations among children of the same age, even variations among children from the same culture.

Making meaning in new ways

Choosing to study something that has purpose and/or special relevance has led teachers we know to gain new understandings about ideas or practices that were already "learned" before. This has been a humbling reminder that "what gets taught is not always what gets caught." It is a reminder, too, that learning can be cyclical, take place on many levels, and often needs time for digesting.

Teacher researcher Emma Markarian's experience offers a good example. When she was student teaching in her teacher preparation program, she conducted a study of balanced literacy. Although she had taken her program's two required literacy courses (which involved extensive field work experiences), she felt that these were not sufficient for her to absorb the theories fully and put ideas into action. So she conducted a study of balanced literacy to help her make sense of what she had learned in her courses. Only after the deep probing of her own investigation did she acquire the "hooks" she needed on which to hang the knowledge she had been introduced to in her classes. Balanced literacy finally made sense to her after that.

A similar thing happened to Patricia, an early childhood teacher who was frustrated with the lack of involvement of the parents of the children in her class. Even though she had taken her teacher education program's required course about family/child/school and was a working single mom who struggled herself to maintain involvement in her children's education, she did not have a perspective on the hardships involved and couldn't understand why others did not do for their children what she did for hers. Not until she conducted her own investigation of parent involvement did she gain a bigger picture and deeper understanding of the challenges/needs of parents and the kinds of partnerships that schools need to create with their students' families and communities. Through the family interviews that she conducted for her study, Patricia developed a better understanding of their life circumstances that made school participation difficult. She stopped blaming the parents for not caring, and began asking *them* for suggestions about how they might be involved. As a result, many parents offered her ideas about how home/school connections could be strengthened. She tried their suggestions and was thrilled to find that many more parents began participating:

> Before this research I blamed parents for not caring. Now I understand better what families are facing. I put myself in their shoes.

Affirmation

An unanticipated, but pleasant outcome for teachers who have engaged in research about their own questions has been finding affirmation for ideas and practices that were previously intuitive. Teacher researcher Jeanette Tavarez, a dual-language teacher, had this happen for her when her study of her program's impact on her students gave support to her anecdotal perceptions about all the ways dual-language programs help children learn language from each other, learn about each other's cultures, and gain respect for each other's differences. She wrote about this in the conclusion to her study:

> Putting together all the pieces of this study has reaffirmed my own educational philosophy and has become a written testament to the overwhelmingly positive benefits that come from enrolling a child in a dual-language program.

Experiencing oneself as a learner

Many teachers we know have changed the way they teach after experiencing themselves as learners in a new way as a result of developing and exploring their own questions. Teacher researcher Seung Hee, a recent immigrant whose schooling was made up primarily of rote learning, credits her research experience with changing her own way of learning and her teaching.

> My experience with research challenged me to learn differ-
> ently. I had to think rather than spit back information. I had
> to generate my own questions and find answers that were
> not already written in books. I was awakened to a whole
> new world of questions, of discovery, of understanding. Now
> I want to do the same for my students.

Reflecting about the research process, trying to make mental notes about what aspects of research feel motivating or uncomfortable, is good preparation for how to provide similarly challenging experiences for our students. Remembering our own experiences can foster empathy with our students if they get overwhelmed in their learning. We, like our students, have now been in similar situations.

Motivation for learning

For some teachers, exploring an issue of personal interest has been a powerful motivator to further learning. Mercedes, who completed a study of how to support the emotional life of children in her classroom, found this to be true:

> I really lived this study. It touched my heart. Exploring
> something that was of personal interest, motivated and
> challenged me. And because of this I gained confidence
> and learned a lot.

This understanding of how learning is supported by building on interests has direct relevance to our work with children. Becoming responsive to the interests and needs of our students can enable us to better support their learning. Teacher researcher Hilda Brito, who did an examination of the impact of her school's partnership with a museum, explained:

> This research process is a model for how to teach children.
> The experience gave me an opportunity to pursue a topic
> that I felt passionate about, and that really made a differ-
> ence. I was really involved in it because it was something I
> cared about. So this has been a good example to me as a

teacher—how whatever I teach has to be connected to children's interests, not merely imposed on them. And then there will be a lot of learning.

Insights like these can be energizing. Teacher researcher Estelle Cadiz, who did a study on how children can be supported as parents go through divorce, elaborates:

> The things I've learned during my research I want to continue. I feel so excited. I don't want to lose this feeling.

Changed attitudes and practices

The research experience has transformed some teachers, changing their attitudes as well as their practices. Michael, whose study of discipline led him to realize that discipline was about building community, not about reacting to negative behaviors in the classroom, details some of how he has changed his teaching as a result of his research:

> Now I let children have a say in what goes on. If they feel that they have ownership of their classroom, they are much more likely to care for it and feel good about being there. I have the room arranged so that it is attractive to the students as well as functional. I have routines in place that are familiar to the students, and this adds to a more calm and stable environment. Transitions are a priority in planning my day. They are critical to the creation of a smooth school experience. I make sure that limitations are set and that everyone knows what they are. Children feel safe when they know there are limits and rules to protect them, and any good community protects its citizens.

And Yolan's inquiry about death and dying led her to change her thinking and her teaching:

> In my first year as a teacher, I remember flushing a dead fish down the toilet and replacing the fish with a look-alike before the children came in. My assistant and I were very young and were not aware of the learning implications of allowing the children to observe the dead fish. As a result of my study of death, I strive to make my classroom rich with experiences with nature. Now, I would never hide a dead fish

from my students. Instead, I would incorporate such an experience into my curriculum. Helping children to understand the natural life cycle can provide them with the prior knowledge to make sense of death if and when it does occur. I am sure to encounter other families with children who have lost loved ones. This study has provided me with the experience to help such families get through the difficult times.

Self-efficacy and possibility

Research about a personal burning question has, for many teachers, fostered their self-efficacy and given them a sense of possibility that they never had before. Teacher researcher Marlene Streisinger was affected by her research in this way:

> Research is like a new pair of good leather shoes; they hurt in the beginning but gradually take on the shape of your foot. As a result of learning to do research, I am much more confident of what I want to do and how I want to do it as a learner. Now I think that my learning is MINE. This is not a dress rehearsal.

Teacher researcher Anna Hart's study helped her to feel more empowered about her own learning:

> I have learned that if you have a question or a problem in your classroom, there is always a way to resolve it. You can find it through research. I never thought it would be possible for me to create my research. But I did. The process has helped me to understand that it is never too late to correct anything in our lives because teaching is a continuous learning experience.

Another teacher researcher imagined possibilities for herself that she never dreamed of before:

> This experience of doing research has greatly impacted me. I feel differently about myself as a learner. I now feel that if you just try, you can do what you want; you can reach your goals and expectations. Most of all I have learned that there is nothing impossible if you put your mind and heart to whatever you do. This changes the way I think about my

everyday work with the children in my classroom. I have learned that all children too have the ability to achieve, and I am just one tool to help them succeed educationally. Every day is the day to make a difference.

Becoming part of a professional community

Some of the teachers we know have found that the research they conducted about their own teaching has led them to a new awareness of what it means to be a professional. Teacher researcher Gina Joseph's study on children's art led her to realize the importance of continuing her learning:

> There is so much to learn in the field of education. The best educators strive for more information and want to find out what research is currently supporting. This experience with research has led me to understand that learning never ends; that there is much to explore. I strive to be an even more well-rounded and well-read teacher, aware of current research and best practices.

Making new beginnings

T. S. Eliot once said: "What we call the beginning is often the end. To make an end is to make a beginning. The end is where we must start from."

The first experience of teacher research is often an end to an old way of teaching—one in which the teacher has all the answers that the students must digest. Teacher research can be an introduction to a new way—one that awakens questions, engages interests, provides resources, and facilitates learning.

For some, an experience with research serves as an induction into the profession. In Chapter 8 we told some stories about teachers who, after completing their first studies, joined teacher research groups, presented at conferences, sought certification from the National Board for Professional Teaching Standards, transformed their teaching, and became resources and change agents for their schools. They credit the process of doing their studies as the catalyst for such changes. As Mercedes said:

> My research experience did not end. It continues in my work today.

Being an inquirer in an era of "right answers"

Some might ask how useful it is for teachers to develop curricula that encourages children to pursue their own questions and nurtures independent thinking in the midst of the constraints on teaching brought about by pressures from high-stakes testing. Our response to this question has two parts: One part has to do with values and the other part concerns good teaching.

Although there are tremendous pressures in schools right now to conform to teaching prescriptions and to turn teaching into test prep, the research about how children learn has never been clearer: Individual development varies and good teaching must be differentiated to accommodate these variations. Educators cannot let current policies obliterate these critical understandings. We have a responsibility to stay true to the knowledge about how children learn and to instill in our students the "habits of mind" that enable them continually to question, examine critically, make connections, and apply knowledge in the real world. Teaching children to question has the power to nurture these dispositions. When teachers, too, tap into the power of questions, we strengthen ourselves to speak out for changes against practices or policies that potentially can harm children's lives. This has been the case for Betty:

> Although I work in a school for young children, I did not
> think it was an appropriate setting for early learning, espe-
> cially in literacy. Before I did my study, I already knew in my
> heart that this was the case, but my research gave me a
> structured opportunity to pursue it. After my research I real-
> ized that I had been on the right track all along.

The other reason to keep inquiry alive in our classrooms, despite the challenges it currently presents to teachers, is that the skills of research are the very same skills that are a part of good teaching and learning. Although the focus of questioning may be different when we adults examine our practice than when children investigate different topics, the skills that we both use are exactly the same—questioning, observing, recording, reflecting, analyzing, and connecting new understandings to prior ones. Teachers who know how to do this well are effective at helping children learn. Their problem-solving orientation prepares them to foster authentic learning, no matter the context in which they teach. And students who know how to do this get the benefit of having a critical eye they can use with everything they do. Learning to question and pursue those questions prepares students to navigate not only the current world of mandates and tests, but, more important, the unknown challenges of the future.

Teaching to support children's questions

Now that we have taken you through all the steps of how to do classroom-based research, shown images of both teachers' and students' investigations, and listened to the voices of teachers about the impact their experiences have had on them, we want to share some final thoughts about the kind of teaching that best supports learners to question and engage powerfully with ideas. Whether you are a teacher of children or adults, we hope that these points about teaching resonate with your own experience as a learner and affirm to you the importance of making them visible in your own work with the students you teach.

Pursue meaningful, purposeful questions

Remember, there is no "right" question that will stimulate learning in authentic and powerful ways. The "right" question is determined by identifying learners' interests and offering opportunities to explore them. We urge you to try to find ways, even within mandated curricula, to allow learners to pursue questions that are both meaningful and purposeful.

Provide ample resources for learning

It is critical to bring varied resources into the classroom and to offer children the opportunity to utilize many learning modalities. Students learn best when the curriculum allows for them to learn in different ways. They are best able to express their learning when they are allowed to demonstrate what they know in a variety of ways.

Be a learner right alongside your students

As teachers we do not need to know all the answers to every question our students have. Nor do we need to be at the center of the learning. Rather, when we guide students and model being a learner alongside them, the children themselves are enabled to step forward to support and learn from each other. This allows a learning community to evolve with enthusiasm that can be contagious and inspiring.

Create a community of learners in your classroom

To take the risks necessary for real learning to occur, learners need to feel safe and supported. They need to feel that the work they are doing is *their own work*, that they have someone who can serve as their guide, and that they have others to whom they can turn for support.

You can provide for these needs by creating a sense of community with the students you teach. Do this by offering lots of opportunities for social interaction and collaboration. One way to do this is to divide class participants into groups based on the common themes of their questions. Regularly these groups can meet to update each other on the progress of their research, to share resources, to give feedback to each other, and to probe each other's thinking. Provide them with focusing questions that can be used to guide their discussions. Before sending students off to do their work, model it first with one or two students in front of the entire class.

Try, also, to provide opportunities for students to reflect regularly on their work and on their group process, either in writing or in verbal "go-rounds." At the end of a study, have students make oral and visual presentations to each other and, if possible, to others beyond the class.

Ask lots of questions and reflect back what you hear

Building curriculum around students' questions requires teachers to be careful observers who mirror to students what they think and understand. Aim to be a facilitator who asks probing questions that scaffold learning.

Continually assess what students can do

To conduct studies built around learners' questions, ongoing assessment must be integral to teaching. It is necessary to interact continuously with your students' learning by regularly collecting and reviewing their work, gathering their responses about their learning through response sheets and mini lessons, and paying close attention to comments and questions raised individually and in class meetings. This information is a guide for what to do next to support learning.

Teach for understanding

Take nothing for granted about what students know. Articulate the purposes for everything that you ask them to do. Explain everything from the ground up. Present and go over in detail each element of each assignment and each skill that needs mastering until you are certain that everyone understands. Define standards for performance publicly and in advance, and delineate criteria for how to meet them. These practices will increase the likelihood that all your students progress and do well.

Carefully scaffold the learning process

Another way to increase the likelihood that all your students will experience success as learners is to pace the learning process to respond to your students' developing skills and understandings. One critical aspect of how to do this is to structure assignments so that each builds a piece of the final project. Rather than using assignments as end points, as is the case in traditional grading, consider giving several draft assignments that lead to a final product. Give feedback on these drafts and return them to the students so they can make revisions before they hand work in for an evaluation.

Assessment rubrics attached to assignments can also be helpful guides for learning. When these are accompanied by examples of accomplished work from past students, the rubrics' descriptions will become more meaningful. But again, use these rubrics to evaluate the final product only after it has been worked on extensively and reviewed several times. In this way, assessment can become a process, not an event.

Weave skills and the requirements of standards into inquiry experiences

Utilizing inquiry experiences to help students acquire mandated skills and content can "turn curriculum planning on its head" (Falk & Margolin, 2005). Try to find ways to embed the information and skills required for your grade level in activities related to the pursuit of students' own questions. Use mandated literacy blocks to have children read about the topics of their inquiries. Hold mini lessons, for individuals or groups, to address identified, needed skills as they arise. When it is simply not possible to teach all required content in this way, group studies can be designed to make sure you address standards. Within these you can offer opportunities for individuals to investigate their own areas of interest.

Provide lots of time to let learning happen

Although it may be difficult for students to learn how to develop their own ideas, it is important to be patient and to give children time. Curiosity is a natural part of each of us. It takes time and hard work to relearn what once came naturally. Try to become comfortable at "letting children learn" (Carini, 1987), allowing students to take charge of their own learning while encouraging them to think independently. Be resourceful when using imposed curricula by embracing the messy and sometimes unplanned occurrences that accompany creativity, self-expression, and the quest for understanding. It takes time to awaken questions, time to become comfortable asking questions, and time to learn that answers can be found.

Anything Is Possible

> If you can walk, you can dance. If you can talk, you can sing!
>
> —Unknown

Anything is possible to accomplish, especially when the conditions are right. When we provide opportunities for children to question, to "be curious—to take the time to look closely, . . . to keep on wandering and wondering," we invite them to discover "the secret to wisdom" that the wise woman pointed out to the little girl in Eve Merriam's story quoted at the beginning of this chapter (Merriam, 1991).

When children are given this gift in school, they not only gain knowledge and skills, they also get excited about setting their own purposes for what they do, find pleasure in pursuing their own interests, and delight in taking charge of their own learning. In an analogous way, when teachers discover this "secret to wisdom" they are strengthened in their abilities to pose and solve problems, connect theory to practice, and tackle the ever-changing challenges that never seem to cease to arise in schools. These skills are exactly the kind that effective teachers possess (Carnegie Forum on Education and the Economy, 1986; Holmes Group, 1986; Joyce, 1990; Lieberman, 1986; National Commission on Teaching and America's Future, 1996, 1997).

Although the approach to learning that has been the focus of this entire book is still a relatively new phenomenon, teacher research and curricula built on children's questions promise many possibilities that as yet remain unrealized. We hope that the explanations, examples, and suggestions presented here help you to generate questions for yourselves and facilitate the pursuit of questions for your students. We hope also that you will use the information in this book to embrace yours and your students' curiosity through inquiry.

Involving teachers and students in research is especially important, we believe, because teachers' and students' collective "vantage point, situatedness, [and] materiality" (Greene, 1997, p. 34) can be instrumental in enlarging perspectives, igniting imaginations, and challenging conceptions of the world as it is. Teachers and students are uniquely positioned to ask and find answers to questions of significance, especially questions related to learning.

The world has many questions that need to be asked and many problems that need to be solved. For these questions and problems—and those yet to be discovered—inquiry offers both teachers and students a powerful method for seeking answers. *"And if you don't find all the answers, you will surely find more to marvel at in this curving, curling world that spins around and around amid the stars"* (Merriam, 1991).

References

Anderson, G. L., Herr, K., & Nihlen, A. S. (1994). *Studying your own school: An educator's guide to qualitative practitioner research*. Thousand Oaks, CA: Corwin Press.

Almy, M., & Genishi, C. (1979). *Ways of studying children* (Rev. ed.). New York: Teachers College Press.

Arnold, K. (1995). *Lives of promise: What becomes of high school valedictorians*. San Francisco: Jossey–Bass.

Barone, T. (1995). Persuasive writings, vigilant readings, and reconstructed characters: The paradox of trust in educational storysharing. In J. A. Hatch & R. Wisniewski (Eds.), *Life history and narrative* (pp. 63–74). London: Falmer Press.

Bissex, G., & Bullock, R. (1987). *Seeing for ourselves: Case study research by teachers of writing*. Portsmouth, NH: Heinemann.

Blumenreich, M. (2001). *Writing/rewriting children: AIDS, discourse, and power*. Unpublished doctoral dissertation, Teachers College, Columbia University.

Boehm, A. E., & Weinberger, R. A. (1997). *The classroom observer: Developing observation skills in early childhood settings* (3rd ed.). New York: Teachers College Press.

Bruner, J. (1960). *The process of education*. Cambridge, MA: Harvard University Press.

Burke, C., & Crafton, L. K. (1994). Inquiry based evaluation: Teachers and students reflecting together. *Primary Voices K–6, 2*(2), 2–7.

Burnaford, G. (2001). Teachers' work: Methods for researching teaching. In G. Burnaford, J. Fischer, & D. Hobson (Eds.), *Teachers doing research: The power of action through inquiry* (2nd ed., pp. 49–80). Mahwah, NJ: Lawrence Erlbaum Associates.

Carini, P. (1987). *On value in education*. New York: The City College Workshop Center.

Carnegie Forum on Education and the Economy. (1986). *A nation prepared: Teachers for the 21st century*. New York: Carnegie Corporation.

Chandler–Olcott, K. (2002). Teacher researcher as a self-extending system for practitioners. *Teacher Education Quarterly, 29*(1), 23–38.

Clandinin, D., & Connelly, F. (1995). Teachers' professional knowledge landscapes: Secret, sacred, and cover stories. In F. Connelly & D. Clandinin (Eds.), *Teachers' professional knowledge landscapes* (pp. 1–15). New York: Teachers College Press.

Clandinin, D. J., & Connelly, F. M. (2000). *Narrative inquiry: Experience and story in qualitative research*. San Francisco: Jossey–Bass.

Cochran–Smith, M., & Lytle, S. (1990). Research on teaching and teacher research: The issues that divide. *Educational Researcher, 19*(2), 2–11.

Cochran–Smith, M., & Lytle, S. (1993). *Inside/outside: Teacher research and knowledge*. New York: Teachers College Press.

Cochran–Smith, M., & Lytle, S. (1999). The teacher research movement: A decade later. *Educational Researcher 28*(7), 15–25.

Cohen, D., Stern, V., & Balaban, N. (1996). *Observing and recording the behavior of young children*. New York: Teachers College Press.

Connelly, M., & Clandinin, D. J. (1990). Stories of experience and narrative inquiry. *Educational Researcher 19*(5), 2–14.

Cortazzi, M. (1993). *Narrative analysis*. London: Falmer Press.

Darling, Eliza. (2003). Fifteen self-editing tips for student writers. *Writing Across the Disciplines*. New York: The City College of New York.

Darling–Hammond, L. (2001). Educating teachers for California's future. *Teacher Education Quarterly, 28*(1), 9–55.

Dewey, J. (1963). *Experience and education*. New York: Macmillan.

Dillow, K., Flack, M., & Peterman, F. (1994). Cooperative learning and the achievement of female students. *Middle School Journal*, 48–51.

Duckworth, E. (1987). *The "having of wonderful ideas" and other essays.* New York: Teachers College Press.

Edwards, C., Gandini, L., & Forman, G. (Eds.). (1998). *The hundred languages of children: The Reggio Emilia approach—advanced reflections.* Greenwich, CT: Ablex Publishing.

Eisner, E. W. (1991a). *The enlightened eye: Qualitative inquiry and the enhancement of educational practice.* New York: Macmillan.

Eisner, E. W. (1991b). What really counts in schools. *Educational Leadership, 48*(5), 10–17.

Eisner, E. (1994). *Cognition and curriculum reconsidered.* New York: Teachers College Press.

Elbow, P. (1973). *Writing without teachers.* London: Oxford Press.

Ely, M., Vinz, R., Downing, M., & Anzul, M. (1999). *On writing qualitative research: Living by words* (2nd ed.). London: Falmer Press.

Erickson, F. (1986). Qualitative methods on research on teaching. In M. Wittrock (Ed.), *Handbook of research on teaching* (3rd ed., pp. 119–161). New York: Macmillan.

Falk, B. (2000). *The heart of the matter: Using standards and assessments to learn.* Portsmouth, NH: Heinemann Press.

Falk, B., MacMurdy, S., & Darling–Hammond, L. (1995). *Taking a different look: How the Primary Language Record supports teaching for diverse learners.* New York: National Center for Restructuring Education, Schools, and Teaching.

Falk, B., & Margolin, L. (2005). Awakening the questions within: Inquiry research in an elementary classroom. *Thinking Classrooms, 6*(2).

Feiman–Nemser, S. (2001). From preparation to practice: Designing a continuum to strengthen and sustain teaching. *Teachers College Record, 103*(6), 1013–1055.

Fine, M. (1992). *Charting urban school reform: Reflections on public high schools in the midst of change.* New York: Teachers College Press.

Florio–Ruane, S. (1990). Creating your own case studies: A guide for early field experience. *Teacher Education Quarterly, Winter,* 29–41.

Florio–Ruane, S., & Walsh, M. (1980). The teacher as colleague in classroom research. In H. Trueba, G. Guthrie, & K. Au (Eds.), *Culture in the bilingual classroom: Studies in classroom ethnography* (pp. 87–101). Rowley, MA: Newbury House.

Frank, C. (1999). *Ethnographic eyes: A teacher's guide to classroom observation.* Portsmouth, NH: Heinemann Press.

Freire, P. (1970). *Pedagogy of the oppressed.* New York: The Seabury Press.

Gardner, H. (1983). *Frames of mind: The theory of multiple intelligences.* New York: Basic Books.

Gardner, H. (1998). *Extraordinary minds.* New York: Basic Books.

Geertz, C. (1973). *The interpretation of cultures.* New York: Basic Books.

Gersh, S. (2004). *Teaching with the internet.* Available at *www.schoollink.org/twin/.*

Gilligan, C. (1982). *In a different voice: Psychological theory and women's development.* Cambridge, MA: Harvard University Press.

Glaser, B. G., & Strauss, A. L. (1967). *The discovery of grounded theory: Strategies for qualitative research.* New York: Aldine De Gruyter.

Glesne, C. (1999). *Becoming qualitative researchers: An introduction* (2nd ed.). New York: Longman Press.

Greene, M. (1978). *Landscapes of learning.* New York: Teachers College Press.

Greene, M. (1997). Exclusions and awakenings. In A. Neumann, & P. Peterson (Eds.), *Learning from our lives: Women, research and autobiography in education* (pp. 18–36). New York: Teachers College Press.

Grimmett, P. (1993). The nature of reflection and Shon's conception in perspective. In P. Grimmett, & G. Erickson (Eds.), *Reflection in teacher education* (pp. 5–15). New York: Teachers College Press.

Guba, E. G., & Lincoln, Y. S. (1981). *Effective evaluation.* San Francisco: Jossey–Bass.

Guba, E. G., & Lincoln, Y. S. (1989). *Fourth generation evaluation.* Newbury Park, CA: Sage.

Harste, J. C. (1994). Literacy as curricular conversations about knowledge, inquiry and morality. In R. B. Ruddell, M. R. Ruddell, & H. Singer (Eds.), *Theoretical models and processes of reading* (4th ed.) (pp. 1220–1242). Newark, DE: International Reading Association.

Hatch, J. A., & Wisniewski, R. (1995). Life history and narrative: Questions, issues, and exemplary works. In J. A. Hatch & R. Wisniewski (Eds.), *Life history and narrative* (pp. 113–136). London: Falmer Press.

Holmes Group. (1986). *Teachers for tomorrow's schools.* East Lansing, MI: Author.

Hubbard, R., & Power, B. (2003). *The art of classroom inquiry.* Portsmouth, NH: Heinemann.

Janesick, V. J. (1991). Ethnographic inquiry: Understanding culture and experience. In E. C. Short (Ed.), *Forms of Curriculum Inquiry.* Albany: State University of New York Press.

Joyce, B. (1990). *Change school culture through staff development.* Alexandria, VA: Association of Supervision and Curriculum Development.

Kilpatrick, J. (1925). *Foundations of method: Informal talks on teaching.* New York: Macmillan.

Lamott, Anne. (1994). *Bird by bird: Some instructions on writing and life.* New York: Anchor Books.

Lieberman, A. (1986). *Building a professional culture in schools.* New York: Teachers College Press.

Lincoln, Y. S. (1993). I and thou: Method, voice, and roles in research with the silenced. In D. McLaughlin & W. G. Tierney (Eds.), *Naming silenced lives: Personal narratives and processes of educational change* (pp. 29–50). New York: Routledge.

Lincoln, Y. S., & Guba, E. G. (1985). *Naturalistic inquiry.* Newbury Park, CA: Sage.

Lytle, S., & Cochran–Smith, M. (1989, March). Teacher researcher: Toward clarifying the concept. *National Writing Project Quarterly*, 1–3, 22–27.

Macrorie, Ken. (1988). *The I Search Paper.* Portsmouth, NH: Boynton–Cook/Heinemann.

Malamud, Bernard (1975). The art of fiction. *The Paris Review, 61*(48).

McDonald, J. (1992). *Teaching: Making sense of an uncertain craft.* New York: Teachers College Press.

Merriam, E. (1991). *The wise woman and her secret.* New York: Simon and Schuster.

Merriam, S. B. (1988). *Case study research in education: A qualitative approach.* San Franciso: Jossey–Bass.

Merryfield, M. (1990, April). *Integrating interpretation and description in case study reporting: Constructing dialogues and scenes.* Presented at the annual meeting of the American Educational Research Association, Boston, MA.

National Association for the Education of Young Children. (1986, 1988, 1989, 1997). *Developmentally appropriate practice in early childhood programs serving children from birth through age 8.* Washington, DC: Author.

National Commission on Teaching and America's Future. (1996). *What matters most: Teaching for America's future.* New York: Teachers College, Columbia University.

National Commission on Teaching and America's Future. (1997). *Doing what matters most: Investing in quality teaching.* New York: Teachers College, Columbia University.

New York City Writing Project. (1982). *Writing and learning across the curriculum: Writing to introduce a topic.* New York: Institute for Literacy Studies, Lehman College, City University of New York.

Osborne, R., & Freyberg, P. (1985). *Learning in science: The implications of children's science.* Portsmouth, NH: Heinemann.

Pataray–Ching, J., & Robertson, M. (2002). Misconceptions about a curriculum-as-inquiry framework. *Language Arts, 79*(6), 498–505.

Patton, M. Q. (1990). *Qualitative evaluation and research methods* (2nd ed.). London: Sage Publications.

Piaget, J., & Inhelder, B. (1969). *The psychology of the child.* New York: Basic Books.

Resnick, L. B. (1987). *Education and learning to think.* Washington, DC: National Academy Press.

Resnick, L. B. (2001). *Accountable talk*. Pittsburgh, PA: Institute for Learning. Available: *www.instituteforlearning.org*. Accessed August 18, 2004.

Richardson, V. (1997). Constructivist teaching and teacher education. In V. Richardson (Ed.), *Constructivist teacher education: Building a world of new understandings* (pp. 3–14). London: Falmer Press.

Rock, R. C., & Levin, B. B. (2002). Collaborative action research projects: Enhancing preservice teacher development in professional development schools. *Teacher Education Quarterly, 29*(1), 7–21.

Sanders, J. R. (1981). Case study methodology: A critique. In W. W. Welsh (Ed.), *Case study methodology in educational evaluation: Proceedings of the 1981 Minnesota Evaluation Conference*. Minneapolis: Minnesota Research and Evaluation Center.

Sanford, B. (2004). It all adds up: Learning number facts in first grade. In M. M. Mohr, C. Rogers, B. Sanford, M. A. Nocerino, M. S. Maclean, & S. Clawson (Eds.), *Teacher research for better schools* (pp. 38–48). New York: Teachers College Press.

Short, K. G., & Harste, J. C., with Burke, C. (1996). *Creating classrooms for authors and inquirers*. Portsmouth, NH: Heinemann.

Stake, R. (1978). The case study method in social inquiry. *Educational Researcher, 8*(2), 5–8.

Tierney, W. G. (1993). Self and identity in a postmodern world: A life story. In D. McLaughlin & W. G. Tierney (Eds.), *Naming silenced lives: Personal narratives and processes of educational change* (pp. 119–134). New York: Routledge.

Tomlinson, C. A. (1999). *The differentiated classroom: Responding to the needs of all learners*. Alexandria, VA: Association for Supervision and Curriculum Development.

Vygotsky, L. S. (1978). *Mind in society*. Cambridge, MA: Harvard University Press.

Weber, L. (1991). *Inquiry, noticing, joining with, and following after*. New York: The City College Workshop Center.

Wells, G. (1994). *The meaning makers: Children learning language and using language to learn*. Portsmouth, NH: Heinemann.

Whitin, D., & Whitin, P. (1996). Inquiry at the window: The year of the birds. *Language Arts, 73*(2), 82–87.

Wiersma, W. (1986). *Research methods in education.* New York: Allyn & Bacon.

Windschitl, M. (2002). Framing constructivism in practice as the negotiation of dilemmas: An analysis of the conceptual, pedagogical, cultural, and political challenges facing teachers. *Review of Educational Research, 72*(2), 131–175.

Witherell, C., & Noddings, N. (Eds.). (1991). *Stories lives tell: Narrative and dialogue in education.* New York: Teachers College Press.

Wilson, S. (1979). Explorations of the usefulness of case study evaluations. *Evaluation Quarterly, 3,* 446–459.

Wolcott, H. F. (1990). On seeking-and-rejecting-validity in qualitative research. In E. Eisner, & A. Peshkin (Eds.), *Qualitative inquiry in education: The continuing debate* (pp. 121–152). New York: Teachers College Press.

Yin, R. K. (1984). *Case study research: Design and methods.* Beverly Hills, CA: Sage.

Zeichner, K. M. (1994). Personal renewal and social construction through teacher research. In S. Hollingsworth & H. Sockett (Eds.), *Teacher research and educational reform* (pp. 66–84). Chicago: University of Chicago Press.

$\mathcal{A}$ppendix 1
Recommended Teacher
Research Articles

○ ○ ○

Brankis, N. (2001). Discovering the real learner within: Journal keeping
with second grade children. In G. Burnaford, J. Fischer, & D. Hobson
(Eds.), *Teachers doing research: The power of action through
inquiry* (pp. 121–128). Mahwah, NJ: Lawrence Erlbaum Associates.

"Discovering the real learner within: Journal keeping with second grade
children" by Nancy Brankis (2001) provides an example of research findings shared in the first person, in chronological order, with examples and
documents from the classroom that illustrate the changes she saw in her
students over time. Woven into Brankis' findings are her experiences as
a teacher and researcher quoted from her research journal.

Compton–Lilly, C. (2003). *Reading families: The literate lives of urban
children.* New York: Teachers College Press.

In *Reading Families,* Catherine Compton–Lilly (2003) examines how the
parents and children in the community in which she teaches conceptualize reading. This book is helpful in the clear way that Compton–Lilly
describes her research methodology and choices as a teacher researcher.
She describes the findings in terms of themes and supports them with
quotations from her classroom, interviews with parents and students, and
field notes.

Csak, N. L. B. (2002). "What's important when you're six?" Valuing children's oral stories. *Language Arts, 79*(6), 82–91.

This article by Nancy Csak describes her examination of what first
graders talk about when offered opportunities to tell stories about their

lives. The author tape-recorded her students' conversations to learn about their language and cognitive development as well as to learn about how she could become a better listener.

Feldgus, E. G. Walking to the words. In M. Cochran–Smith, & S. Lytle (Eds.), *Inside/outside: Teacher research and knowledge* (pp. 170–177). New York: Teachers College Press.

This article is a description of an inquiry conducted by teacher Ellen Feldgus about how print in the classroom environment supports young children's reading and writing. Through an analysis of her documented observations of the children in her class during their literacy periods, of collections of children's writing samples, and of interviews with the children about their work, the author gains a deeper understanding of how children use the print in the environment to further their learning.

Murphy, P. (1994). Antonio: My student, my teacher. *Teacher Research: The Journal of Classroom Inquiry, 1*(2), 75–88.

"Antonio: My student, my teacher" by Paula Murphy (1994) is an account of one teacher's inquiry about how to help a struggling student learn how to read. Through observations of Antonio at school; interviews with him, his family, and his past teachers; and a visit to Antonio's home, the author uncovers information that helps her to understand not only this particular child, but that leads to insights about all children and how better to facilitate their learning.

Sanford, B. (2004). It all adds up: Learning number facts in first grade. In M. M. Mohr, C. Rogers, B. Sanford, M. A. Nocerino, M. S. Maclean, & S. Clawson (Eds.), *Teacher research for better schools* (pp. 38–48). New York: Teachers College Press.

"It all adds up: Learning number facts in first grade" (2004) is a chapter written by teacher researcher Betsy Sanford, about developing an instructional plan to teach her first grade students number facts. Sanford shares her research in a chronological narrative, describing first how she introduced her teaching strategy with her students and then providing different themes of what she learned during the process. She clearly describes her original tentative findings and then highlights a central finding in her study.

Appendix 2
Good Sources for Website Evaluation Criteria

○ ○ ○

A WebQuest on Evaluating Web Pages
http://mciunix.mciu.k12.pa.us/~spjvweb/evalwebteach.html

Critical Evaluation Survey
http://discoveryschool.com/schrockguide/evalhigh.html

Cyberguide Rating for Content Evaluation
www.cyberbee.com/guides.html

Evaluating Web Sites: Criteria and Tools
www.library.cornell.edu/okuref/research/webeval.html

Kathy Schrock's Information about Evaluating Web Resources
http://discoveryschool.com/schrockguide/eval.html

The Web—Teaching Zack to Think
www.anovember.com/articles/zack.html

Why It's a Good Idea to Evaluate Web Sources
http://lib.nmsu.edu/instruction/eval.html

$\mathcal{A}$ppendix 3
Handy Little Guide for
Referencing in APA Format

○ ○ ○

In anything you write it is often common to reference the ideas or the actual words of others. It is important to recognize when you are doing this and always to give credit to the originator of the idea or the author of the words. Sometimes the ideas you are using have a history that has been developed over the years by numerous thinkers. In such cases it is important not only to give credit to all those who have had a role in shaping the ideas, but you also want to make clear to your reader that your ideas are connected to them.

Even if, for right now, you think that your study will be used only for your own purposes, citing references is a good habit. It is easy to lose track of who said what, what ideas and words are yours, and what came from others. As you progress with your study, you may find that you want to share it with other colleagues at conferences, in workshops, or in articles. For this, you *must* credit the originators of the words or ideas you have used through references and it is much too difficult to track down the citations after the project is completed.

There are numerous referencing styles used across the different disciplines: APA (American Psychological Association) format, Modern Language Association (MLA) style, or Chicago style. Because APA style is commonly used in many areas of educational research and writing, reference guidelines are provided here for that. For more comprehensive coverage and details, please consult the *APA Manual,* 5th edition or the APA website *(www.apastyle.org/elecref.html).*

There are two types of referencing you need to do when writing anything that uses the ideas or words of others: references within the text that credit the author whose ideas or words you are using and end-of-text references that list complete information about the published works from which you have obtained the ideas or words.

In-text references

There are two types of credits that must be given within the body of a text: when you use the important ideas of others and when you use the actual words of another author in a quote.

Quoting an author

If you use someone else's words you must provide information right after the quote about whom you are quoting, the date the author's words were published, and the page number of the publication in which the words appeared. The citation information should be in parentheses. If the quote is only a sentence or two, it can be within the body of the text enclosed with quotation marks. Here is an example:

> The proliferation of standards creates demands that are increasingly difficult to meet. "The Mid-continent Regional Educational Laboratory has even estimated that it would take 6,000 extra hours of classroom time to cover all the information required on most state standards, roughly the same amount of time that it takes to earn a master's degree." (Stoskopf, 2000, p. 38)

When quoting material that is longer than one or two sentences, you still need to provide an in-text citation in parentheses, providing information about the author, date of publication, and page number, but instead of using quotation marks, you indent the quote in the text. Here is an example of a quote (an extract) that should be indented in the text rather than surrounded with quotation marks:

> Education is of critical importance. W. E. B. DuBois expressed it well:
>
> > Of all the civil rights for which the world has struggled and fought for 5,000 years, the right to learn is undoubtedly the most fundamental ...the freedom to learn ...has been bought by bitter sacrifice. And whatever we may think of the curtailment of other civil rights, we should fight to the last ditch to keep

open the right to learn, the right to have examined
in our school not only what we believe, but what
we do not believe; not only what our leaders say,
but what the leaders of other groups and nations,
and the leaders of other centuries have said. We
must insist upon this to give our children the fair-
ness of a start which will equip them with such an
array of facts and such an attitude toward truth
that they can have a real chance to judge what the
world is and what its greater minds have thought it
might be. (DuBois, 1949, pp. 230–231)

Referencing an idea

If you are discussing an idea or information that you have learned from
another author or authors, it is also important that you credit that author
or authors in the text after the idea. Here is an example:

> In Nigeria, by the age of five, children can sing hundreds of
> songs, play numerous instruments, and perform dozens of
> complex dances (Armstrong, 1987).

Please note that when you are referencing an idea in the text, you do
not need to provide a page number, just the author's last name and date.

End references

All the references you have made within your text need to be listed with
complete information about where they can be located at the end of
your writing. This list should include all the sources you have consulted.
The best way to keep track of these is to start creating your reference list
when you begin reading. Every time you use someone else's ideas or
words, write down the following information:

Author

Title of the publication

Date of the publication

Volume and issue if the publication is a journal

Place of publication and publisher if the text is a book

Page range

If you do this you will not have to retrace the information later.

There are lots of little details to which to pay attention when you are creating a reference list. The list should be arranged in alphabetical order by the author's last name or, if there is no author, by the first word of the title of the article you are citing. Citations vary depending on whether the text is a book, an article in an edited book or reference book, an article in a periodical, a technical or research report, a revised edition, or a multivolume work. Although the differences in how to cite different kinds of references may seem trivial (and indeed they are, compared with the *quality* of your thinking and your writing), it is important to know what is expected in the profession and to be able to meet these expectations. The following is a brief summary of some of the main rules (not at all inclusive) for how to do end references in APA style:

- Double space all entries.
- Indent all lines by one tab after the first line.
- List all authors alphabetically, by last name.
- Type all authors' names with the last name first followed by a comma and then the full names or initials of the authors' first and middle names.
- If there is more than one author, use the symbol "&" to connect the authors rather than the word "and."
- If the author is also the publisher, put "Author" where the publisher's name should go.
- If the author has more than one work referenced, cite the earliest work first.
- Use sentence case for the titles of books and articles (i.e., begin the first word of the title with a capital letter but use lowercase for all subsequent words in the title, except for proper nouns or the first word after a colon, which should also have a capital letter).
- Capitalize the first letter of all words in the title of a journal.
- Italicize the title of books, and the title and volume number (not the issue number) of journals.
- Place parentheses around the issue number of journals.
- Do not underline or put quotation marks around the title of articles.

- Provide the place of publication followed by a colon and the full name of the publisher.

- Use the abbreviation "p." or "pp." before page numbers in books, magazines, and newspapers, but not for scholarly journals.

- Separate each section of the reference with a period followed by two spaces.

The following are some examples:

One author
Arnold, K. (1995). *Lives of promise: What becomes of high school vale-dictorians.* San Francisco: Jossey–Bass.

Two or more authors
Cohen, D. H., Stern, V., & Balaban, N. (1997). *Observing and recording the behavior of young children* (4th ed.). New York: Teachers College Press.

Group author
National Commission on Teaching and America's Future. (1996). *What matters most: Teaching for America's future.* New York: Author.

Unknown author
Americana collegiate dictionary (4th ed.). (1995). Indianapolis: Huntsfield.

Edited volume
Cohen, D., McLaughlin, M., & Talbert, J. (Eds.). (1993). *Teaching for understanding: Challenges for policy and practice.* San Francisco: Jossey–Bass.

Article or chapter in an edited book
Chittenden, E., & Courtney, R. (1989). Assessment of young children's reading: Documentation as an alternative to testing. In D. S. Strickland & L. M. Morrow (Eds.), *Emerging literacy: Young children learn to read and write* (pp. 107–120). Newark, DE: International Reading Association.

Notice how the editors of the book in which the article or chapter appears are listed in this kind of reference with their first and middle initials first.

Article in a journal

Cooper, E., & Sherk, J. (1989). Addressing urban school reform: Issues and alliances. *Journal of Negro Education, 58*(3), 315–331.

Journals generally have one volume per year and produce monthly or quarterly issues for each volume. Although many journals list both volume and issue (as done in this example), some list only the volume and demarcate the issue numbers only by numbering their pages continuously from one issue to the next.

Article in a magazine

Simmons, H. (1995, November 29). Changing our buying habits. *American Consumer, 21,* pp. 29–36.

Article in a newspaper

McDermott, M. (September 2, 1999). Board enforces test practice. *The Riverdale Press,* p. A3.

Unsigned newspaper article

New study promises age-defying pills. (1995, July 27). *The Washington Post,* p. B21.

Unpublished paper

Trimble, K., & Sinclair, R. L. (1986, April). *Ability grouping and differing conditions for learning: An analysis of content and instruction in ability-grouped classes.* Presented at the annual meeting of the American Educational Research Association, San Francisco, CA.

Internet citation

If you find an article on-line from a print source and it is posted exactly as it appears in print, cite the reference as you would a print source but place [electronic version] after the title:

VandenBos, G., Knapp, S., & Doe, J. (2001). Role of reference elements in the selection of resources by psychology undergraduates [electronic version]. *Journal of Bibliographic Research, 5,* 117–123.

If you read an article on-line but suspect it has been altered for the on-line version, use the following format. Please make sure to put the date that you retrieved the article, because the content of the website may change, be revised, or be removed:

> Cotton, K., & Reed–Wikelund, K. (2001). Parent involvement in education. *Regional educational laboratory.* [On-line]. 1–8. Available: *www.nwrel.org/scpd/sirs/3/cu6.html.* Accessed May 14, 2002.

Or, if the source is only an on-line source, put as much information as is supplied (author if there is one, year, and the title of the article), followed by the date accessed and the Internet address. If the author of a document is not identified, begin the reference with the title of the document.

A useful free site to help you format your references is The Citation Machine at *www.landmark-project.com/citation_machine/cm_web.php3.* It provides a form for the needed citation information for different kinds of texts. You fill in the correct information, choose in which format you want the citation to appear (APA format, the MLA format, or Chicago style used by some of the social sciences) and it then organizes the information correctly. It is not foolproof, however. You *do* have to watch out for certain details that the Citation Machine does not take care of. For example, if you capitalize the entire title of a book (even though APA style does not), the Citation Machine will not "uncapitalize" the words. So, be sure you are doing citations correctly. You still need to learn the basics of the style.

$\mathcal{A}$ppendix 4
Sample Literature Review
by Natalie McCabe

○ ○ ○

As an early childhood teacher, one has to wonder how there could possibly be a debate about the need for play in the lives of young children. However, some educators, administrators, and legislators, to this day, fail to see the important role that play can have in the life of a child. Studies in the field of education have found ample evidence of the important role that play, dramatics, and accessibility of materials can have on the development of the learner (Nel, 2000). Questions arise about how best to foster and facilitate age-appropriate play in classrooms. I have found ample studies and arguments in support of play. There are several main subjects discussed in the articles and books I read that I found useful:

1. Play affords opportunities for development.
2. The teacher has a crucial role in facilitating play.
3. Imagination is expressed and developed in dramatic play.
4. The arrangement and maintenance of the learning environment is crucial to support the children best.
5. Children exhibit a natural affinity for play.

The articles I found argue for the importance of appropriate, child-initiated, teacher-facilitated play (Bradekamp, 1997).

Play affords opportunities for development
There is no doubt in the minds of child researchers that play is a tool for the development of a child's emotions, social behavior, vocabulary, and motor skills (Bradekamp, 1997). Skills modeled and used in play

will eventually become tools children can use in "nonplay situations" (Johnson in Christensen & Kelly, 2003, p. 528). I find this to be particularly interesting having worked with a rigorous standardized curriculum like "Success for All." In "Success for All," the children are taught too many new concepts one after another and are not given the appropriate time to reflect on what they have learned. Play is a great way for children to react to and process what they are learning. Boyer (1997–1998) finds that not only will children who have been given time for appropriate play be able to work better with others, they will be more willing to take risks and go beyond the context of a situation. I hope to see instances when my children are extending their learning into play situations as I conduct my study.

Monighan–Nourot et al. (1987) offer three specific developmental processes in children's play that are important to address. The three processes that children go through in play are contextualization, decontextualization, and recontextualization. In contextualization, the child is beginning to see other perspectives and actually beginning to use some physical objects symbolically. This is the beginning of play as an intellectual experience for the young child. In decontextualization, the child is not only able to use objects symbolically, but s/he can distance herself from the play enough to take on a dramatic role as well (Monighan–Nourot et al., 1987). I found in my kindergarten this year a few of my English-language learning students were more hesitant with this process, clearly because of vocabulary deficits, but also because of a timidness to let go dramatically as they may never have done at home. Watching other children in the class assign them roles and more or less direct them into the drama is an interesting scaffolding process entirely done by the children as they begin to conceptualize what it means to pretend play. Finally, this idea of recontextualization is the way young children find ways to bring in themes or experiences they have in solitary play into group play (Monighan–Nourot et al., 1987). This is evident in classroom play because children are excited to share experiences they have had. This helps them to play cooperatively because they get to take turns introducing new elements into their dramatic situations, while at the same time reflecting in a way they might not otherwise have an opportunity to do. I think these three developmental processes accurately depict what children are doing in scenarios I have seen play out in my class, and they are only one part of how play affords opportunities for development for the whole child.

Emotional development

As far as emotional development, Nel (2000) sites some work done by child development theorist David Elkind, in which he finds that the language that comes from play can actually help children cope with their emotions. The importance of child-initiated play is crucial here, particularly to show that children can bring in whatever feelings they are having about their home life into play in the classroom as a mechanism to cope (Nel, 2000). The fact that children will use skills from play to deal with real-life situations in contexts other than the classroom environment is the first evidence of its importance. In my study, I will be interested to see times when I learn more about the home life of my students by observing their play conversations and the situations they act out.

Cognitive development

Neumann (cited in Sponseller, 1974) attempts to summarize Piaget's theories on play in *Play as Learning Medium*. She explains that play is how children manipulate the outside world to fit their own cognitive schema (Neumann in Sponseller, 1974). This makes sense in the context of a lesson for a kindergarten class. The teacher gives a mini lesson, models some strategy on the rug, perhaps even has a few children come up to demonstrate said strategy in front of the group, but in order for all the children in the class to feel that strategy at work, they have to use it on their own. Once they are allowed to play with it or manipulate it, be it a new word or a new concept for reading or writing, they can make it a part of their own schema. Piaget describes children moving along a continuum from the development of symbolic thought, to understanding games with rules, to eventually the point where play becomes an intellectual activity (Neumann in Sponseller, 1974). Cognitively, children cannot simply be receptors of knowledge, hence the movement away from standardized whole-group instruction to active, individualized early childhood classrooms. Children must be allowed the opportunity to develop understandings of rules and intellectual thoughts in relation to games and the other play activities they incorporate (Neumann in Sponseller, 1974).

Bergen (1988) also elaborates on the many cognitive strategies demonstrated when children play, such as planning, problem solving, and goal setting. With symbolic thought and role playing comes skills related to negotiation and interactive dialog that, for many children, are a new experience. They develop an ability to improvise during play, which is something they will need for the rest of their lives.

When implemented properly, Christensen and Kelly (2003) find that play helps to build vocabulary as children become curious and begin to question the tools in their environment. It is also very key for English-language learners as another way to communicate (Christensen & Kelly, 2003). Boyer (1997–1998) finds that a child who develops a playful outlook in life can approach situations with less fear. The teacher can work with the students to apply new vocabulary and strategies to different scenarios, making connections in the process. Play should be a comfortable and natural part of the learning and discovery process with the help of an effective teacher.

The teacher has a crucial role in facilitating play

Although some teachers do set aside a block of time for "play" or "centers," Christensen and Kelly (2003) argue this is not the most developmentally appropriate type of play. To maximize student learning and development, Christensen and Kelly (2003) suggest "high-level play," in which children use materials more effectively to solve problems. The teacher is not just sitting aside watching the children freely explore the materials, but he or she plans specifically what types of materials to set up and what types of scenarios to suggest. This certainly does depend on the age of the child. The readings have focused on the preschool and kindergarten years. A teacher of children this age is guiding them, helping them to extend their play and keep it productive. Although independence is, of course, ultimately encouraged, the teacher, by adding or taking away materials, suggesting roles, or even suggesting a switch in the plot of a dramatic scenario, is acting to scaffold what the children have already begun. It is crucial that the teacher allow the children to maintain ultimate control to remain motivated (Bergen, 1988). Play needs time to flourish and develop, and it is hard under time constraints to allow children to stop and explore something they find interesting throughout the course of learning. I was a teacher who had a specific block of time for learning center play and I watched as the children simply did not have enough opportunities to develop their play. Now that balanced literacy is being introduced, I am seeing how learning center play incorporated throughout the day and coupled with free play and exploration really allows the students to flourish in the active learning environment.

According to Christensen and Kelly (2003) play can be facilitated in two crucial areas: manipulatives and dramatic play. With teacher guidance, the children should be using materials for higher order thinking, problem solving, and developing new understandings. One example of how a teacher could acceptably facilitate learning from high-level dramatic play is by suggesting certain roles for the children to take on, to experiment with. Using their knowledge and observations of societal roles, the children will act out behaviors and vocabulary dramatically. Scaffolding the children by helping them retell, discussing the setting of a scenario, and placing props in the center is the role of the effective play facilitator (Christensen & Kelly, 2003).

In answering the question of why a teacher should intervene in play, Monighan–Nourot et al. (1987) find that not only should the teacher model, take anecdotal records, and explore the whole child, but he or she should make time for personal reflection on his or her pedagogy. I think this is an important point that may be overlooked. In order for a teacher to be a truly great facilitator of play in the classroom, it is imperative that he or she looks at this as a creative learning process from the pedagogical side as well as for the developing child. I am trying with my teacher reflective journal to allot a few minutes each day to write about things that happened in the classroom, things that went well, or things that I could change or elaborate on. I think the teacher must allow for change and accommodate for personal learning discoveries made throughout the time teaching.

Along these same lines of the role and responsibility of the teacher, is what I read in *Play as Medium for Learning and Development: A Handbook of Theory and Practice*, which emphasized that the most powerful strategy for a teacher is preparation, organizing the physical setting and materials (Bergen, 1988). Particularly at the beginning of a school year, the teacher's choice of materials and room arrangement are important, because the children will be relying heavily on the physical objects offered to them. Once their symbolic thought develops to a higher level, they'll be capable of more serious manipulation, but it is crucial for the teacher to think through the purpose and the role that lessons serve in developing learning.

Imagination is expressed and developed in dramatic play

To begin a discussion on imagination in play, I find the description given in the book *Play as a Learning Medium* to be useful. In this book, put out by the National Association for the Education of Young Children (NAEYC), the definition of the word *medium* is addressed as found in Webster's dictionary. It is found to be a "condition in which something may function or flourish; "a channel of communication" or a "material or technical means of active expression" (Webster's dictionary in Sponseller, 1974). What an accurate way to establish how play works to facilitate the expression, development, and use of a child's imagination. When children become comfortable with the freedoms that play affords them, only then will they truly be using their creativity and stepping into their imaginative selves.

Some find that sociodramatic play assists in literacy development, and this is largely related to the theories of Vygotsky, who found that the sociocultural context of children's cognitive development is of the utmost importance (Vygotsky in Korat, 2003). The child uses pretend play as a way to develop language, relationships, and other higher mental functions. If the teacher supportively designs areas in the room where the children's dramatic play can flourish, then the children are going to elaborate on what is given to them and what they know. Korat (2003) gave the example of an Israeli kindergarten where the teacher set up an "office corner" with a few simple supplies, such as a phone and typewriter, and she observed as the children began to run their own office and choose a subject, a theme, develop vocabulary, and work cooperatively. Given some simple props, the children were able to use their own imaginations to elaborate on the scheme (Korat, 2003). The teacher can continue to provide them with challenges and support.

Boyer (1997–1998) discusses the work of Valett, who found that children use their sensory impressions and experiences to develop symbolic representation. The teacher should offer children a variety of ways to use materials, she should encourage discussion of how certain sensory experiences make them feel, and she should encourage kids to think of how they are using their senses in play (Boyer, 1997–1998).

Bodrova and Leon (2003) write about the importance of increasing the amount of time we allow children to reflect on and absorb the information we teach them. Play serves as a time when they can experiment with symbols, ideas, and relationships that are not entirely tied to any particular context (Bodrova & Leon, 2003). They need the opportunity not only to think about what they have learned, but to apply it to different contexts in a comfortable environment where they feel they can take risks and be creative.

Arrangement and maintenance of the learning environment
Nel (2000) emphasizes that the reading area must be cozy, the art center engaging, and print and writing must be promoted through a variety

of means to ensure engagement on multiple levels by all learners. Nel (2000) also discusses how teachers must model play behaviors for the children using the materials and extending beyond the concrete concept of materials. So although play will certainly occur naturally among children, the teacher should be considering the optimal ways to design an environment conducive to active play. I hope to implement some of these strategies and watch as my children become more comfortable and more willing to take risks in our classroom.

Children exhibit a natural affinity for play

"Play is seen as the child's natural curriculum" (Monighan–Nourot et al., 1987, p. 138). I think this statement is powerful and true. It describes the fact that in any early childhood setting, the community is made up of a bunch of little people eager to learn, eager to touch and explore, and armed with limitless energy to think and act on what they experience. Play is simply the vehicle to act on this eagerness and this energy they bring to school. In describing the characteristics of behavior that is play, Monighan–Nourot et al. (1987) site five different characteristics, three of which specifically address the point that children have an innate affinity to play. During play, the child must be actively engaged, there exists some kind of intrinsic motivation for the play, and the attention is to the means, rather than the ends (Monighan–Nourot et al., 1987). Children at a young age are the most curious of all learners. They must be engaged and participating in their learning and, really, they must have a say in what and how they are learning for their experience to be optimal. It is important for teachers to be open to an emergent curriculum, one that they develop based on the students' curiosities, which allows for the children to demonstrate and then elaborate on their interests. Through play, the teacher sees what the children want to explore when given the freedom of time and the support of materials.

Children are naturally anxious to figure things out on their own. I watched my children this year experiment with colors. I put out only primary-color crayons at the start of our kindergarten year and it was not long before the children were discovering that blue and yellow made green and red and blue made purple. It was natural for them to use the materials I had laid out in creative ways, and they were making learning discoveries on their own. I could have just told them what would result from mixing colors, but it was not only important to give them time with the materials on their own, but more so, to allow them the freedom to be their own teachers. Play is often the doorway to learning concepts that teachers far too often simply "teach."

Boyer (1997–1998, p. 90) sites some work done by Lieberman in 1977 that suggests "playfulness" is a style of play that enhances and develops the child's natural inclination to learn. Children quite naturally have curiosities about the daily experiences they have, and they need opportunities to question, explore, and develop freely. Playfulness naturally encourages children to think and act in terms of their feelings, and playful children tend to be happier (Boyer, 1997–1998).

Christensen & Kelly (2003) find teachers must take advantage of the fact that children come in with experiences, understandings, and wonderings about the world around them. Play that is built on these familiar concepts can draw out all children. One suggestion is to take a community walk to explore familiar surroundings in a new way and then to come back and reflect on the trip through play (Christensen & Kelly, 2003). Nel (2000) stresses the importance of building on the child's interests, which occur innately in every scenario. Each child who goes on the field trip may notice something completely different. Sharing these discoveries and building on them in future lessons is key to maintaining appropriate play (Nel, 2000).

Conclusion

After reading these articles it seems such an obvious injustice that there are still plenty of educational establishments that dispute the validity of play in the lives of young children. All the articles and books I read find that play allows children to develop a self-awareness and self-regulation crucial for nonplay tasks. Boyer states that playfulness "allows children to develop self-awareness as well as control of environmental objects, their movements, and their bodies" (Boyer, 1997–1998, p. 92). I hope to discover, over the course of my study on play in centers, how a teacher can best foster independent learners through play. I am lucky to have a principal who is very supportive of facilitated play. Children come into school armed with curiosity, energy, and natural inclination toward play.

There is research being done about the importance of play, and I am curious to show through my observations and my own reflections that play is a crucial part of an early childhood curriculum. A teacher who plans strategically can truly maximize development across the spectrum of social, emotional, physical, and cognitive behaviors by thinking critically about the role of play for young children.

References

Bergen, Doris. (1988). *Play as a medium for learning and development: A handbook of theory and practice.* Portsmouth, NH: Heinemann.

Bodrova, Elena, & Leon, Deborah J. (2003). An hour of play—what for? *Scholastic Early Childhood Today, 17*(5), 5.

Boyer, W. A. R. (1997–1998). Playfulness enhancement through classroom intervention for the 21st century. *Childhood Education, 74,* 90–96.

Bradekamp, S. (Ed.). (1997). *Developmentally appropriate practice in early childhood programs.* Washington, DC: National Association for the Education of Young Children.

Christensen, Ann, & Kelly, Kim. (2003). No time for play: Throwing the baby out with the bath water. *The Reading Teacher, 56*(6), 528–530.

Korat, Ofra. (2003). Sociodramatic play as opportunity for literacy development: The teacher's role. *The Reading Teacher, 56*(4), 386–393.

Monighan–Nourot, P., Scales, B., and Van Hoorn, J. (1987). *Looking at children's play: A bridge between theory and practice.* New York: Teachers College Press.

Nel, E. M. (2000). Academics, literacy, and young children: A plea for a middle ground. *Childhood Education, 76*(3), 136–141.

Sponseller, D. (Ed.). (1974). *Play as a learning medium.* Washington, DC: National Association for the Education of Young Children.

$\mathcal{A}$ppendix 5
Related Resources

○ ○ ○

Cochran–Smith, M., & Lytle, S. (1993). *Inside/outside: Teacher knowledge and research.* New York: Teachers College Press.

Fletcher, R. (2003). *A writer's notebook: Unlocking the writer within you.* New York: HarperTrophy.

Fletcher, R. (1999). *Live writing: Breathing life into your word.* New York: Harper Trophy.

Frank, C. (1999). *Ethnographic eyes: A teacher's guide to classroom observation.* Portsmouth, NH: Heinemann.

Freeman, D. (1998). *Doing teacher research: From inquiry to understanding.* New York: Heinle and Heinle.

Goswami, D., & Stillman, P. (Eds.). (1987). *Reclaiming the classroom: Teacher research as an agency for change.* Portsmouth, NH: Boynton/Cook.

Hobson, D., & Smolin, L. (2001). Teacher researchers go online. In G. Burnaford, J. Fischer, & D. Hobson (Eds.). *Teachers doing research: The power of action through inquiry* (2nd ed., pp. 83–118). Mahwah, NJ: Lawrence Erlbaum Associates.

Hubbard, R. S., & Power, B. M. (1999). *Living the questions: A guide for teacher researchers.* Portland, ME: Stenhouse.

Hubbard, R. S., & Power, B. M. (2003). *The art of classroom inquiry: A handbook for teacher–researchers* (Rev. ed.). Portsmouth, NH: Heinemann.

Lamott, A. (1994). *Bird by bird: Some instructions on writing and life.* New York: Doubleday.

Lincoln, Y. S., & Denzin, N. K. (2003). *Turning points in qualitative research: Tying knots in a handkerchief.* New York: AltaMira Press.

Meyers, E., & Rust, F. (Eds.). (2003). *Taking action with teacher research.* Portsmouth, NH: Heinemann.

Mills, G. E. (2003). *Action research: A guide for the teacher researcher.* Upper Saddle River, NJ: Merrill Prentice Hall.

Short, K. G., Harste, J. C., with Burke, C. (1996). *Creating classrooms for authors and inquirers* (2nd ed.). Portsmouth, NH: Heinemann.

Zerubavel, A. *The clockwork muse: A practical guide to writing theses, dissertations, and books.* Cambridge, MA: Harvard University Press.

Internet resources

Assembling a list of works cited:
www.lib.duke.edu/libguide/works_cited

Guide to writing research papers:
http://cctc.commnet.edu/mla/index.shtml

Teacher research site: *http://gse.gmu.edu/research/tr/*

Teacher resource site: *www.landmark-project.com*

ndex